Be Blessed in What You Do

The Unity of Christian Ethics and Spirituality

by
Michael K. Duffey

Paulist Press ♦ *New York* ♦ *Mahwah*

Copyright © 1988
by Michael K. Duffey

Library of Congress Cataloging-in-Publication Data

Duffey, Michael, 1948–
    Be blessed in what you do / Michael Duffey.
      p.   cm.
    Bibliography: p.
    ISBN 0-8091-2960-4 (pbk.)
    1. Christian life—Catholic authors. I. Title.
BX2350.2.D83 1988
248.4'82—dc19

88-2405
CIP

Published by Paulist Press
997 Macarthur Boulevard
Mahwah, New Jersey 07430

Printed and bound in the
United States of America

Contents

Acknowledgments

This book was written over several seasons, always along with other academic responsibilities. Progress was aided one summer by a grant from the Andrew W. Mellon Foundation and another by a summer faculty fellowship from Marquette University. I would like to thank two people for their continual encouragement during the project—my friends Dr. Stanley Hauerwas and Br. Robert Smith, who read and commented on the manuscript at various stages. I am also grateful to Camille Slowinski for her faithful typing of parts of the text. Mr. David Schimpf ably assisted in final proofing. I would also like to acknowledge the encouragement offered me by Mr. Douglas Fisher of Paulist Press. Although our children John, Teresa and Elizabeth could not yet read as this was being written, I know that their joyful, exuberant, attentive and trusting way of living and loving has taught me much along the way.

This book is dedicated to Mary Beth, in gratitude for her encouragement and interest. My summers were easier because hers were not. My prose is better because of the clarifications she offered. The ideas herein were nurtured by the insights she offered during those few moments parents find for such things. Most of all, her attentiveness to the spiritual depths and riches of her life and our life together has filled my heart and work.

Dedication

to Mary Beth

Introduction

"Love one another." We have heard this advice before. We wish that we could love others and live in peace with them. Yet we have been wounded by the love others have withheld or by our attempts to love that have been rebuffed. We have also heard the advice to "just be yourself." It is well-intended but does not comfort us when we fear how others will receive us. Loving others, and knowing and accepting ourselves—these seem to be two of life's hardest tasks. In fact, we must be able to do both if we are to accomplish either one. And both are related to yet another task, the quest to know God. The love command which Jesus gives us contains all three: we are to love God and love our neighbor as we love ourselves.

Knowing God, knowing ourselves, and being capable of love are fundamental to our existence. Thomas Merton, an American Christian monk, wrote:

> There is only one problem on which all my existence, my peace, and my happiness depend: to discover myself in discovering God. If I find Him, I will find myself and if I find my true self I will find Him.[1]

1

Merton described the consequences of not knowing God:

> People who know nothing of God, and whose lives are
> centered on themselves, imagine that they can only find
> themselves by asserting their own desires and ambi-
> tions and appetites in a struggle with the rest of the
> world. They try to become real by imposing themselves
> on other people, by appropriating for themselves some
> share of the limited supply of created goods and thus
> emphasizing the differences between themselves and
> others who have less than they, or nothing at all.[2]

Recognizing the presence of God in our lives and recognizing our relatedness to God enable us to love one another.

This book is about ways of self-discovery and of love as
they are understood in the Christian tradition. In theological terms, this book is about the necessary relationship between Christian moral theology and Christian spirituality.
"Spirituality" is a word with a wide range of meanings.
While we will speak of it at greater length below, here we
may define "spirituality" as the human movement toward
the God revealed to Israel and through Jesus Christ that is
manifested in greater wholeness of life through communion
with others. The theme in all that will be said about spirituality and morality is their relatedness. Our moral lives are
part of a spiritual quest. Spirituality is the companion of
moral development.

For the past several centuries a common perception
has been that Christian morality and spirituality are very different activities. Although the two great commandments,
love of God and love of neighbor, unite spirituality and
morality, the notion arose that two qualitatively different
vocations existed within Christianity that reflected different
capacities for love. Those relatively few who were called to

religious life were viewed as pursuing lives of greater holiness; the laity living "in the world" were encouraged to do God's will in this world in the hope of being rewarded with the vision of God in the next. In such a two-tier Christianity, "spirituality" was relevant mainly to those in "religious life." The laity's religious obligation was reduced to the avoidance of moral failure. Too little attention was given to the knowledge and love of God as the source of our power for loving each other. Indeed, the strength to love depends upon the experience of love, which for Christians is in one way or another the experiencing of the God who *is* Love. Spiritual and moral life are about God's self-gift: the encounter with Love and the enactment of love. Too often Christians have come to view the moral life as something less. When Christian morality seems only to counsel us to be "minimally decent" Samaritans, the moral life degenerates into a minimalistic strategy to keep on a straight and narrow path and prevent the ultimate disaster of forfeiting eternal life. And spirituality is regarded as a luxury which might be pursued only after the prior, "preventative" task of morality has been attended to.

Today there are hopeful signs of renewal of moral theology. Interest in the moral significance of the scriptures, in the faith and moral development of persons, and in the social responsibility of the Christian community reflects that renewal. Recognition that Christian morality is a response to the divine grace and holiness offered to humankind through Jesus Christ suggests that morality and spirituality are being reunited. All of it recognizes that the Christian moral quest to love the neighbor is intimately related to our quest to know and love God. But the process of renewal continues.[3]

Every Christian is called to be a source of God's love in the world. But to be so we must come to know who we are.

The spiritual call is neither the vocation of a few elite Christians nor the privatizing of faith that leads away from the world. Instead it is the call of all people to bring the quest for self-knowledge and for community with others to completion through the encounter with God.

In our search for a unified Christian spirituality and morality we begin with Jesus, who said to his disciples in words of farewell, "Love one another, as I have loved you" (Jn 14:34). Chapter One begins with Jesus Christ, whom Christians worship as the fullness of God's grace and power and as one whose love makes our love possible. With those who directly encountered Jesus, we are called to be his followers, submitting ourselves to the power of God as Jesus did to become instruments of God's healing love and justice in the world. We will see that it is often in the hours of our own deepest crises and personal defeats that we do meet the Christ and are given new hearts for the adventure of following him where we would otherwise be afraid to go. The Epistle to the Colossians directs us to be transformed by Jesus, to "put on a new self which will progress toward true knowledge the more it is renewed in the image of its Creator" (Col 3:10).

Chapter Two explores Christian spirituality in terms of the gradually unfolding recognition of the power of God working through the stages and seasons of our lives. We will consider how we might be more receptive to being refashioned by God, by learning to give up some of our control and wait for God. Rather than focus on spiritual practices associated with particular religious orders, we will consider the contemplative dimension of every human life. We will consider prayer, not as an activity that temporarily distracts us from the world but as a means of experiencing the presence of God transforming our lives.

Chapter Three seeks an understanding of the Christian

moral life. While it may be understood in somewhat different ways (sometimes as essentially obedience, other times as the pursuit of the good) we will emphasize the Christian moral call as essentially responding to the manifold ways in which God is acting upon and seeking us. To "put on Christ" is to make response to the God of Jesus, to be perfected by responding to the offer of divine friendship. Our present images of ourselves, incomplete and only partly true, must be transformed. Where self-reliance has become our primary virtue, we must reconsider how we will use our capacities for moral agency. Hence, Merton spoke of the faculty of the will in a manner that at first seems odd. He said:

> My will must always be ready to fold back within itself and all the powers of the soul into its deepest center to rest in silent expectancy for the coming of God, poised in tranquil and effortless concentration upon the point of my dependence upon Him; to gather all that I am and have and all that I can possibly suffer or do or be, and to abandon them all to God in the resignation of a perfect love and blind faith in God, to do His will.[4]

To think about ethics is also to think about the way power is used. In Chapter Four we first examine power under the influence of sin which is manifested in various forms of self-deception. We then consider human power as it is transformed by grace, both to break down the walls that divide us, and to form us into a community. The power of God manifest in Jesus is a paradoxical kind of power that submits to the powers of evil in order to defeat sin and death forever. It is through the power of love that God reclaims us and the entire creation for holiness and peace once more.

In Colossians, the effect of becoming new selves in Christ is described in terms of the acquisition of particular virtues:

> You are God's chosen race, his saints; he loves you. You should be clothed in sincere compassion, in kindness and humility, gentleness and patience. Bear with one another; forgive each other. . . . Over all these clothes, to keep them together and complete them, put on love (Col 3:12–14).

Chapter Five describes the virtues the people of God need to sustain them in working for the kingdom. We will illustrate those virtues by observing the lives of real and fictional people (the compassion of Dorothy Day and the Catholic Worker movement; the justice and mercy enacted by Celie in Alice Walker's novel, *The Color Purple*; the hope, courage and patience of Martin Luther King, Jr. and the thousands who struggled non-violently for racial justice in America). Together the virtues give us the power to be a community of friends seeking to bring the world into closer friendship with God.

Together, these chapters seek to connect morality and spirituality, faith and action. They reflect the great desire for Christian renewal that marked the Second Vatican Council. In its various pronouncements the Council affirmed that the entire "people of God" are called to holiness in their various worldly works. Holiness is to be found not in separation from the world but through compassionate presence in it. The distinctions between nature and grace, the natural and the supernatural, no longer delimit the task of the Church and its members. Our conceptions of holiness and worldliness must be brought together.

The spiritual and moral insights of Thomas Merton

(1914–1968) have frequently found their way onto the pages ahead. Merton is the most well-known Christian monk of our time. *The Seven Storey Mountain*, the story of his conversion, and Merton's numerous other writings have had a profound effect on Catholics and other Christians for almost four decades. Merton was a visionary whose own life reflected the renewal of the Christian life in terms of uniting monastic holiness and compassionate worldliness. He continually reminded his fellow monks and all of us living worldly lives that we are marked out as a holy people, remade by God's grace in order that we may remake the world to conform to God's love and justice. Our enthusiasm depends literally on being filled with the power of God. In the face of much fragmentation which daily threatens to pull us apart, the power of the Spirit can teach us who we are. In the face of the temptation to despair of doing anything, the Spirit of Love enables us to take the first step toward love, and the next and the next.

1
Jesus, Alpha and Omega

Introduction

Almost two millennia ago a man named Jesus entered
the synagogue of Nazareth in Galilee and taking the scroll
began to read the already seven-century-old words of
Isaiah:

> The spirit of the Lord has been given to me, for he has
> anointed me. He has sent me to bring the good news to
> the poor, to proclaim liberty to captives and to the blind
> new sight, and to set the downtrodden free, to proclaim
> the Lord's year of favor (Lk 4:18-19; Is 61:1-2).

Declaring that these words were that day being fulfilled, he
set out preaching throughout the countryside of Galilee
how the kingdom of God was at hand. For the Galileans
who heard him, groaning under the oppression of Roman
occupation, the disdain of the religious elite in Jerusalem,
and the apparent disfavor of God, Jesus' words of radical
liberation kindled new hope. At that juncture of the history
of Israel in that apparently forsaken land of Galilee a radical
liberation of the human spirit was being born. Into Israel's
search for God came Jesus inviting Israel to live as though

God alone reigned and to seek after and bow down before no other power than God's.

Something happened to those who encountered Jesus. Something continues to happen to all those generations of people who experience Jesus. In some fashion or other, the encounter with Jesus is felt to be the fulfillment of the promise made by Yahweh through the prophet Ezekiel five centuries before Jesus' coming:

> I will give them a single heart and I will put a new spirit in them; I will remove the heart of stone from their bodies and give them a heart of flesh instead. . . . Then they shall be my people and I will be their God (Ez 11:19–20).

In this chapter we reflect on the power of the encounter with Jesus. We do so by asking two questions as we survey the scriptural testimonies of those who were among the first to have the experience of Jesus. First, who were most open to Jesus' proclamation of the kingdom? Who took new heart in his words? Second, what sort of change did the encounter produce in their lives? These questions are obviously not prompted only by historical interest. We ask them as people who desire to "take heart" in Jesus more deeply, that by undergoing a greater depth of conversion we may have new hearts for following him as his disciples.

1. The Kingdom and the Cross

To understand Jesus as the one who reveals the truth about God, who gives us new hearts and leads us to the fullness of life, we begin with the testimonies of those who were among the first to be transformed by Jesus. Who were they and what had they heard and seen? Those with hearts most open to Jesus' words and way of life were the *anawim* of Israel, those "poor in spirit" whose lack of power, status, or wealth made them willing to trust him. Jesus told them: "The time is fulfilled, and the kingdom of God is at hand. Repent and believe the Good News" (Mk 1:15). They came to understand Jesus' preaching about the "kingdom of God" as the revelation of the intention and character of God. They were enabled to believe that God providentially cares for all of the creation and desires that its original goodness be restored. God's reign is found where justice and compassion shine through human behavior. By teaching in parables Jesus suggested the hiddenness of the reign of God, comparing it to the tiny mustard seed that will one day become an enormous tree and to the yeast now hidden in the dough that will soon leaven it. The reign of God is an invitation to a way of life which human beings must consciously choose.

The fitting human response to the kingdom is to stop whatever else one may be doing and earnestly commit oneself to discerning the will of God. Jesus' parables stress putting the kingdom first, responding like a man willing to sell all he has in order to buy the precious pearl he has discovered (and not responding like those who spurn invitations to a great wedding feast). The urgency of Jesus' message implies a warning: those who refuse God's just and compassionate reign will be lost. But the message is preeminently one of hope: repentance is possible because God is boundlessly forgiving and compassionate. The decisiveness of response is suggested in the Gospel account of Jesus' choosing of the Twelve. Unquestioningly and unhesitatingly they left whatever they were doing and followed him.

The Gospel stories about Jesus' activities indicate that what people heard Jesus say they also saw him enact.

Leander Keck observes that Jesus aligned himself so fully to the will of God that he was "permeated by the kingdom of God." Jesus brings the kingdom, Keck continues,

> not to impart correct concepts about the kingdom but to make it possible for men to respond to it; as a parable of the kingly God, he invited men to look through him into the kingdom, with the result that his hearers could not respond to the kingdom without responding to him.[1]

By the example of Jesus' own trust he invited others also to trust in the providence of the God he called "Abba"— Father. His miraculous cures of those spiritually and physically afflicted announced that the compassionate reign of God had come. He evoked astonishment not because he was capable of magic but because in him people were grasped by the compassionate presence of God breaking into the world to heal human brokenness. To those who responded to Jesus (whom an early Christian writer called the *autobasileia*, the kingdom in person) wholeness and fullness of life were at hand.

Jesus' life was a parable of the power of God. In his touch was the power of love which reconciled and reunited. He rejected power that took the form of controlling and subjugating others and securing wealth and privilege for oneself and one's "own." "The fact that Jesus pointed to and preached the Kingdom without calling attention to himself," Stanley Hauerwas observes, "is but an indication of the kind of rule he brings."[2] Jesus was unmoved by the pretensions or offer of any power that sought to rival God's, as the story of his temptation in the desert illustrates. The power to which he was loyal—and which was the source of his power—was manifested in acts of consoling, forgiving, and reconciling human beings. Through such power the yoke of oppression was lifted and the compassion of God was felt.

What did it mean for those whom Jesus encountered to take his teachings "to heart"? What sort of response did he inspire in them? The New Testament attributes to Jesus no systematic ethical teaching. It suggests instead the moral imperative of imitating Jesus and with him testifying to the presence of the kingdom of God. Jesus exhibits the virtues of the kingdom: trust and obedience, boundless compassion, forgiveness, and refusal to hate even one's persecutors. His followers were to do likewise. By the experience of his compassion they were enabled to repent of their sins and to live according to the rule of such compassion. The *anawim* took heart in Jesus, writes Monika Hellwig, because

> he overcame blindness, deafness and hardness of heart in people . . . encouraged them out of their paralysis, loved them out of their panic and confusion, released them from crippling physical and psychological burdens, brought them back to life. But the Gospels also tell us that the principal concern of Jesus was to refocus and re-educate their imagination. Legalism, superstition, lack of basic self-worth and the pervasive, crippling fear of a generally oppressed consciousness, seemed to have cramped and withered their power to image God or their own future or the possibilities of their own present society. And this paralysis of imagination was evidently projected onto God as the harsh judge and taskmaster, as the distant one who no longer granted the gift of prophecy or the present revelation of his wisdom and purpose in the world.[3]

All of this is what believing in and being redeemed by Jesus meant.

Not everyone, of course, responded to Jesus' invitation. Because Jesus challenged their authority the religious leadership in Jerualem reacted strongly against him. Mark records that while many experienced Jesus as the source of new hope, those who wielded power over the people were fearful of the freedom he offered to them and labeled his claim to forgive sins "blasphemous" (Mk 2:7). To them, Jesus' message of freedom spelled revolt and they conspired to be rid of him (Mk 3:6). From almost the beginning of Mark's Gospel, readers are being prepared for Jesus' fate. Three times Jesus foretold what would happen to him and instructed his disciples on the personal cost of being his followers:

> Anyone who wishes to be a follower of mine must leave self behind; he must take up his cross, and come with me. Whoever cares for his own safety is lost; but if a man will let himself be lost for my sake and for the Gospel, that man is safe (Mk 8:34–35).

Indeed, the religious and political powers prevailed against him. He was arrested, falsely accused and unfairly condemned, tortured and crucified.

Those who had found their hopes newly kindled by Jesus were indeed utterly disheartened by his death. Mourning and fearful, his disciples went into hiding. On the third day two of them met a "stranger" on the road to Emmaus and lamented how their hopes that Jesus "would be the one to set Israel free" had been dashed (Lk 24:21). The full range of the shock at the death of Jesus and the seeming abandonment of God is suggested by Rowan Williams:

Those who at first believed in Jesus of Nazareth as God's delegate had to resolve the appalling paradox that the fulfiller of God's Law had been condemned and killed. . . . If God is to be seen at work here he is indeed a strange God, a hidden God, who does not uncover his will in a straight line of development, but fully enters into the world of confusion and ambiguity and works of contradictions—the new covenant which both fulfills and radically alters the old, the Messianic age made real amid the suffering and failure of the present time.[4]

In their encounter with the risen Jesus, however, their despair over his death is transformed into a hope beyond hope.

Those who have experienced all of this now took heart in Jesus as never before. As C.H. Dodd writes, Jesus' rising from the dead

was the rebirth of the people of God, the rising of Israel from the dead. . . . The darkness and desolation of Good Friday and the miserable sabbath which followed it had emptied life of all meaning for them. On the "third day" they "were raised to life with Christ," as Paul put it; and that is a confession of faith hardly less basic than the proclamation, "Christ is risen."[5]

The empty tomb marks a beginning. As the angel declares, "He is going on before you into Galilee; there you will see him, as he told you" (Mk 16:7). Together, Jesus' way of life, his submission to death, and his resurrection announce the presence of the kingdom of God.

"Taking to heart" the message of Jesus required that those seeking to imitate Jesus' acceptance of the kingdom had to understand the meaning of his cross. The resurrection revealed to them that Jesus had been raised to incomparably "new" life—and had given them reason to hope for such life—by submitting to the cross as the final chapter in a life of boundless compassion. As Jesus' dedication to others had known no limits, now his glorification by the Father was total. Mark's Gospel draws the intimate link between Jesus' glorification and his passion, underscoring the proleptic presence of God's reign in the darkest hours of Jesus' life. The kingly imagery of Jesus being "crowned" with thorns, robed in royal purple, and "enthroned" between two thieves all anticipate his full glorification. Together Jesus' death and resurrection affirm God's dominion over sin and its fruit, death.

Jesus' death and resurrection give Christians new courage. Jesus' submission to sin signals God's binding up of brokenness in the very midst of Jesus being broken. Jesus frees us from the fear of death so that we may take fully to heart the work of imitating his compassion. The "good news" of Jesus now also included the "hard news" that giving oneself over to the reign of God meant that disciples of Jesus must be willing to suffer as he did at the hands of those whose power is threatened.

As Jesus had no illusions about the consequences of trusting God and daring to carry the kingdom message of compassion and forgiveness across all class and party lines, those who proclaimed him to be their risen Lord could not refuse with their own lives to pick up the cross and follow him in the course of their own lives. Their crisis over his death was resolved in a new level of insight and hope into God's saving power. They could now "take to heart" Jesus' message by risking to extend compassion in his name, even when to do so was to be deemed scandalous and to invite suffering and rejection. Yet many did follow him, proclaiming that the kingdom of love had come through his very humiliation and would continue to come through theirs. With St. Paul they said with confidence:

> We proclaim Christ—yes, Christ nailed to the cross; and though this is a stumbling block to Jews and folly to Greeks, yet to those who have heard his call, Jews and Greeks alike, he is the power of God and the wisdom of God (1 Cor 1:23-24).

Indeed the claim was scandalous for Jews and Gentiles alike. For the former it was irreligious to claim that the Messiah had been humiliated and crucified; for the latter it was irrational to believe that this peasant from obscure Palestine was divine. Jesus' disciples knew how offensive (and seemingly contradictory) it was to preach Jesus' divinity and his humiliating rejection. Some of the particulars of his life only made it worse: Jesus had befriended tax gatherers, prostitutes, and the physically and mentally afflicted. He had shown great kindness for those most suspect in terms of the keeping of the Jewish law—literally, for the "outlaws." But Jesus' followers knew what power flowed from the encounter with this man.

We raise the issue of the "scandal" of the Christian profession because Jesus as the revelation of God may be as scandalous to us as to our "Greek" and "Jewish" predecessors. The perennial danger is that Christians themselves will prefer a "different" Jesus whose relation to them is less demanding. While saying that "we believe" in Jesus "born of the Virgin Mary" who "became man" and was "crucified under Pontius Pilate," we may turn away from the bloodied face of Jesus because of its implications for us as his disciples. There are a variety of ways in which we may seek to remake him in our own image instead of allowing ourselves to be remade in his. We may ignore his historical

particularity—that is, the social, political, and religious history into which he fit—as irrelevant for our time. We may
even deny Jesus' genuine humanity, considering it unseem-
ly that God should participate in our "soiled" existence.
From the very beginning Christians have had to remind
themselves that the profession that "Jesus is Lord" is a profession of the divine presence in his manner of living and
dying as well as in his resurrection. Christians are called to
seek God by imitating Jesus rather than by hoping to experience the divine outside of history and the flesh.

The image of the bloodied Jesus remains a scandal. We
are tempted to look past his cross because of its implications for our own lives as believers. We must acknowledge
the cross and recognize our need to penetrate its meaning.
As Thomas Merton reminds us,

> It is useless to study truths about God and lead a life
> that has nothing in it of the Cross of Christ. No one can
> do such a thing without, in fact, displaying complete
> ignorance of the meaning of Christianity.[6]

Christians find God where they least expected: in agony
upon a tree. In Jesus' death, the seeming destruction of
meaning becomes the possibility of new meaning. We are
forced to rethink how God is God. Paul's profession that
Jesus, living in the vulnerability of the flesh and dying in the
indignant manner of a criminal, was the "image of the unseen God" was unacceptable for many. But for those who
did receive him, he was to open a new way to God. For
them the death of Jesus on the cross redirected their search
for God and opened a new way to God.

The greatest threat to the Christian profession of Jesus
comes not from those who refuse to acknowledge his divinity. Instead, it occurs whenever Christians are tempted to

turn Jesus into merely a proposition, an idea, or an ideal rather than a particular person who announced the kingdom in a particular social and political milieu and invites us to do so in ours. Only by seeing how and why Jesus offered a radical alternative to the religious and political arrangements within *that* world can we begin to appreciate his radical challenge to ours. Jesus' revelation is vitiated when he is made out to be some "best version" of ourselves and our society as we presently understand them. For as the one we worship as the "image of the unseen God," Jesus is radically different from us. But he invites us to be like him by urging us to abandon all sources of security other than God and by reassuring us that repentance and reform are possible because his and our Father is infinitely forgiving. His liberating message and presence is the offer of our restoration in God's image. By attending to his particular life we see into the kingdom and are given hearts for doing his work.

Jesus, in all of his particularity, is the grounding of our moral and spiritual aspirations. James Gustafson writes that the moral life of the Christian community

> is in its fullest sense a way and a pattern of life for those whose faith in God has Jesus Christ at its center. It is not first of all a universally valid objective model of morality. This it may provide, but only as an expression of God's ways to man in Jesus Christ.[7]

Jesus is normative precisely because he embodies the ways of God. In his deeds and preaching we come to see Jesus as the power of God transforming the world. His teaching and healing specify how the power of God transforms hearts, minds and bodies. When we can affirm that a momentous event of grace occurred through a humble Jew in an ob-

scure place two millennia ago, then we are fertile soil for
Jesus' momentous announcement: "Repent, the kingdom
of God is upon *you*" (Mk 1:15). Hauerwas sees disclosed in
the Christian profession of Jesus the essence of the Christian moral life:

> We are called to be like God: perfect as God is perfect,
> like this man whom God sent to be our forerunner in
> the Kingdom. That is why Christian ethics is not first of
> all an ethics of principles, laws, or values, but an ethic
> that demands we attend to the life of a particular indi-
> vidual—Jesus of Nazareth. It is only from him that we
> can learn perfection—which is at the very least nothing
> less than forgiving our enemies.[8]

Both our moral and our spiritual ways of life depend for
their fruitfulness on the experience of Jesus, giver of new
life and hope. His life and message sent the seeds of the
kingdom blowing down the centuries, as it were. We are the
soil in which the kingdom is to take root and grow. His
death offered us new freedom to practice compassion, to
take up his cross in order that his seed might grow into a
rich harvest. Jesus has given us not only his life and death
but also his Spirit for the task of being remade in the divine likeness.

Now almost two millennia after Jesus announced and
enacted God's offer of salvation, he continues to invite us to
conversion. Such can only happen if we desire to know
Jesus. Thomas Keating speaks of the necessity of knowing
Jesus and of the self-transcendence to which such knowledge leads.

> The key to being a Christian is to know Jesus Christ
> with the *whole* of our being . . . to know his sacred
> humanity through our senses and to reflect upon it with

our reason, to treasure his teaching and example in our imagination and memory, and to imitate him by a life of moral integrity. But this is only the beginning. It is to the transcendental potential in ourselves—to our mind which opens up to unlimited truth, and to our will which reaches out for unlimited love—that Christ addresses himself in the Gospel with particular urgency.[9]

The familiar terms "repentance" and "conversion," often used too glibly, involve no less than "going down into the chaotic waters of Christ's death," there to "surrender to the pattern of sacrificial torment and death."[10] Let us consider further the matter of conversion to fuller life with Jesus.

2. Jesus Beckons Us

Conversion is the transformation which Jesus effects in his followers. The Hebrew Scriptures describe conversion as the turning away from idols and a returning to Yahweh. Such a process is, in Ezekiel's words, the trading of hearts of stone for hearts of flesh. Jesus urged on his hearers repentance in the form of setting their hearts on the kingdom. Theologian Rosemary Haughton describes conversion as the "life-long process . . . in which all personal gifts and virtues are swallowed up, transformed in a love which is not our own, yet is most surely one's real self."[11] Let us reflect on what happens in the process of conversion by considering the transformation that occurred in the life of St. Paul and in the life of a Christian contemporaneous with us.

St. Paul tells the story of his conversion in his letters of encouragement to others who, like him, are young in their faith. To the Christians at Philippi he describes his life both before and after his encounter with the risen Christ on the road to Damascus. "I was a Hebrew born of Hebrew parents," he writes, "and as far as the law can make you perfect, I was faultless" (Phil 3:5-6). But Paul now reckons his former uprightness of life as a "disadvantage" in light of "the supreme advantage of Christ Jesus in my life" (Phil 3:7-8). The distinction which Paul would often make between observing the Jewish law and gratuitously experiencing the grace of Christ is rooted in his own experience. Having experienced the latter he now seeks only "to know Christ and the power of his resurrection and to share his sufferings by reproducing the pattern of his death" (Phil 3:15). Paul speaks of being "captured by Christ" in order that his hidden self might grow strong by being inhabited by Christ and so be perfected (Phil 3:13, 16ff). So powerful is Paul's transformation that he refers to the condition of his present life as being lived by Christ: "Now I live, yet not I, but Christ lives in me" (Gal 2:20). His only way to express what has happened to him is to say that Christ lives in him.

The effect of Paul's encounter with Jesus is not to seek withdrawal from the world but to give himself to doing the work of Jesus. His conversion leads him to seek participation in Jesus' way of life and to accept Jesus' way of death. Such a journey of participation in Christ's life and death is signified by one's baptism into the Christian commmunity, as Paul tells the Christians at Rome (Rom 6). To the Philippians he writes: "I am caught in this dilemma: I want to be gone and be with Christ, which would be very much the better, but for me to stay alive in this body is a more urgent need for your sake" (Phil 1:23-24). Paul recognized that the faith he had come to possess could not grow apart from a community in which to share it. He became a tireless apostle, founding and nurturing numerous communities. Paul's concern for the way of life of the community reminds us that if our encounter with Christ is authentic it must lead to service that builds up the entire "body of Christ." For

Paul, to "put on Christ" meant to become a holy people. He exhorted the Roman Christians: "Offer your bodies as living sacrifices, holy and acceptable to God" (Rom 12:1).

Though Paul's conversion was dramatic and radical, we see in his encounter with Christ three effects that mark the fullness of all Christian conversions. First, Paul's experience of Jesus made him yearn for a more total union with him. Second, Paul sought the company of those who have come to the knowledge of Christ (and, by his tireless apostleship, built up such community). Third, on account of the potent love he had experienced in Jesus, Paul became a channel of divine compassion for others.

If this is what happens in the course of conversion, how does the process begin? Drawing on the testimony of St. Paul, Haughton distinguishes (and relates) the human and the divine movements of the conversion process. She describes the human preparation as a "formation" process in which the Christian community gives its members some experience of mutuality, empathy, and trust in the hope that they will become fertile soil for the gratuitous divine initiative—the "transformation"—by which human beings are freed to be radically loving and trusting. The gap between formation and transformation cannot be bridged no matter how earnest the desire from our side. Haughton notes the great paradox in the relationship between our formation and the transformation God effects in us. Our desire is indeed critically important; yet, we often cease to desire God by being content with our own goodness. We recommit ourselves to seeking God when we acknowledge that our formation (and any formation) is hopelessly insufficient to make us into what we need to become.

Haughton illustrates the formation-transformation process by telling the story of a contemporary conversion that has much less drama about it than Paul's. It is worth recounting some of the details of the story to appreciate the transformative power of encountering Christ now as then. Haughton's illustration involves a middle aged man in the midst of what is often termed a "mid-life crisis." The man's life situation, which plays an important part in precipitating his crisis, she describes in the following way. He is married and has one daughter in her early twenties. His emotional investment as both husband and father has dwindled to being very little. He has accomplished a modest amount of professional success but his relationships with his colleagues, as with his wife, have yielded little more than minimal amicability. In short, whatever passion for anyone or anything he once experienced has now faded. What currently is generating some emotion—in the forms of frustration and distress—is his increasing alienation from his daughter, who has recently become active on behalf of the poor of their city.

In the face of his daughter's self-commitment and her zeal for a cause, the lukewarm character of his own existence becomes increasingly distressing. For a while he seeks a way out of his increasing pain by trying to get involved in her and her friends' activism. But he soon loses heart. His desire for his life to have some new meaning and mooring yields none. He is adrift and now more consciously and painfully aware of it than ever before. His loneliness deepens as he no longer seeks the company of his daughter's activist circle that briefly gave him a sense of purpose and made him feel connected. One night, mildly intoxicated and en route home from a bar which he has begun to frequent, he is injured in an auto accident and hospitalized. Lying in the hospital bed, his loneliness and self-loathing are overwhelming. The crisis of his life is now at full strength. As Haughton describes it, "the normal structure of security, the life of the world, seem no longer safe or even very real."[12]

The man continues in this state until one night a nurse gives him a New Testament tract which for lack of anything else to occupy himself he begins to read. Suddenly, in the gray twilight a breakthrough happens which will set him on the road of repentance and conversion. He is suddenly made aware that he is loved—as if he was remembering something that he had once known as a child, but had long forgotten as an adult. The love he has experienced is that of Jesus Christ. Haughton's description is worth quoting at length:

> He encounters Christ as the one who cares, who wants him. The Christian idea of conversion is that whatever the circumstances and people concerned a real conversion is a conversion to Christ and in Christ. . . . An idea of Christ may come over with extraordinary vividness, either because he is eloquently described, or because even a trite description, as in this case, is encountered in circumstances producing sensitivity. If the vision that is conveyed does have this impact the reaction is as great as that to any encounter with great love. It is greater than most because any account of Christ must show him as *above all loving*. His is a heroic self-giving, without condition or limit. If people can respond to real love even from a comparatively selfish person, it is not surprising that they respond to the love of Christ, once the idea of his love ceases to be a phrase in a sermon and becomes a personal reality.[13]

The man is filled with this love—this compassion with which Jesus has cured countless others before him—and is changed radically by the experience. This "dark night" becomes for him a night of grace.

In the crisis of human failure and the awareness that we lack completely the power to ensure a meaning for our lives we can only entreat God to come to us and fill the deep void within with love. "Transformation" refers to the breaking into our lives of divine love which enables us to be with others through experiences of self-giving love without fear of self-loss. Then "decent" relationships can give way to self-giving ones. It is not that God can only work on adequately formed human beings. But it would be hard to discern the invitation to a more exacting love if we knew nothing of what minimal regard for others amounted to. Likewise, in the wake of a transformation, what we have seen, felt, and been able to do "in Christ" must become part of the continuous formation of the community of believers.

Haughton makes two observations about the conversion process she has illustrated. First, she notes that like all converts he now feels himself obliged to carry out the commands of Christ:

> This time he does not have to wonder what he is committed to, or rely on a vague feeling that he ought to change more than his evening occupations. In the light of his new self-discovery he knows where his failures have been and therefore what he—not anyone else at all but just he himself—needs to do about it.[14]

Second, what the man still requires is the support of others to understand more fully what has happened to him and with whom he can celebrate it. That is, he needs a community to deepen and renew his transformation. It would be a serious distortion in the account of this man's experience to omit what is likely to follow for him, or Paul, or anyone. Living as we are "between the times" of Jesus' cross and his glory, the times are still perilous. Those who have been transformed must still tend to their (and others') formation and must still face the possibility of failure and despair.

What we have described is Paul's and a more ordinary (though fictitious) Christian's conversion in which Jesus is seen to be both initiator and ultimate end. Hearing and telling the stories of Jesus' invitations to the kingdom and of his healings is a reminder that *we* are being invited to be healed and transformed. The biblical stories and the stories later Christian communities tell are stories involving us since we, too, are being beckoned by Jesus. We cannot say when or how or under what circumstances Jesus Christ will reveal himself to us and transform our lives. In whatever the form it comes it will be an encounter with the person of Jesus. We will not merely have grasped an idea of God but will have encountered someone who calls us to be his disciples. We will have been grasped by a power which inspires not fear but the movement of love in our lives.

3. Discipleship

In later chapters we will focus on Christian morality as the desire to live as Jesus' disciples. In the ancient world the nascent Christian movement was referred to as "the Way," reflecting its insistence that belief in Jesus required committing oneself to a way of life imitating his life. "The Way" suggested a pattern of behavior marked by love of neighbor— and special concern for the poor and weak, joyful hope in Jesus' return, and deep confidence in the providence of God. "The Way" might also remind Christians that they are on the way: they cannot stay where they are but must go forward with Jesus. Jesus' life continues the journey motif that began with the story of Abraham and Sarah leaving their kin and venturing to a country Yahweh would show them (Gen 12). Like them, Jesus' self-realization required that he leave the familiar and be led into strange places in order to accomplish his mission. Jesus' journey took him to the desert, into the unfamiliar countryside (into Samaria where he startled a Samaritan woman by asking her to draw water for him, a Jew), and finally to Jerusalem with its religious elite and Roman occupiers. Jesus urges his disciples to go with him to the next town to "preach there also; for that is why I came out" (Mk 1:38). In the final verses of the Gospel of Matthew Jesus exhorts them to go out and "make disciples of all nations" (Mt 28:19).

For Christians, discipleship is a journey in a twofold sense. It is a journey out of ourselves to befriend the stranger. It is also a journey toward the discovery of our authentic selves. Jesus told his disciples that henceforth their "kin" will be all who do the work of the Father. Jesus went out to people whom his fellow Jews regarded as strangers, befriending, for example, a Samaritan woman. Paul went to the Gentiles. We witness in the early followers of Jesus the welcoming of strangers and the creation of communities. Rather than remaining with "our own kind," occupying self-imposed ghettos, we are called to go out to others, to minister to the stranger.

Living amidst "strangers" in a foreign place often teaches us (not without some pain) about how much we share in common with others. American theologian David Burrell reflected on his sojourn in Israel, where he lived among Jews and Muslims. There he came to recognize that Jews, Christians, and Muslims all respond "to a call, the call originally issued to Abraham, to come out of one's own familiar land into one which the Lord will give us."[15] Addressing especially his fellow American Christians, he continues:

> It is the shape of that call which is new for us today, and as the call changes so must our response. The call of us Westerners is to step out of our presumed supremacy

and to allow ourselves to become part of a new constellation of peoples and cultures which will literally change the face of the earth. It was that man of remarkable inward response, Thomas Merton, who put his finger on it and embarked on the corresponding journey when he met his death. He wanted to become, he said, a "universal man." That is, he wanted to shed those layers of presumption that took Western culture and the Christianity which had grown up with it, as the paradigm of human achievement.[16]

With extraordinary insight Burrell writes about the constructive alternatives which will help us to come out of our ghettos so that we may be "removed from the familiar, yet eased into reality" where we may attend to others as the good Samaritan did.

The call to be Jesus' disciples is a call out of our present state of self-awareness in order to follow him. This calling forth is the center of our spiritual and moral journeying. The two senses of the call are inseparable, for as Burrell reminds us: "Personal spirituality does not describe a private journey so much as a program which would develop the capacity for relating . . . our inmost self to—all there is!"[17] Responding to the call to come out of ourselves and be possessed by God is the general form of our obedience to Jesus' commands. It is the first movement necessary for God to possess us and bear fruit in us.

The Christian journey to others and to self is the journey with Jesus toward entry into the reign of God. Baptism, symbolizing our willingness to go with him into the ultimate unknown, death, reminds us that we cannot stay where we are but must venture into the unknown with him. He whom we thought we knew when we assented to being his disciples is revealed more fully to us on the journey. We know

him in the love of neighbor. We know him when we take up
his cross. Discipleship is both the fruit of conversion and the
way of deepening conversion. We have the hope of encountering Jesus as those in Galilee once did. For as Albert
Schweitzer wrote:

> He speaks to us the same word: "Follow me!" and sets
> us to the tasks which He has to fulfill for our time. He
> commands. And to those who obey Him, whether they
> be wise or simple, He will reveal Himself in the toils, the
> conflicts, the sufferings which they shall pass through in
> His fellowship, and, as an ineffable mystery, they shall
> learn in their own experience Who He is.[18]

Conclusion

Coming to know Jesus Christ is at the center of the
Christian moral and spiritual journey. The Scriptures reveal
Jesus as the proclaimer of the kingdom of God as well as
the one who exemplifies the appropriate response to it.
Jesus urges his disciples to respond to the kingdom by
imitating him in acts of compassion and healing wherever
human pain and brokenness is encountered. Jesus' unqual-
ified trust in the Father, his hunger for righteousness, and
his love for all—including his persecutors—constitutes for
Christians an "ethic of the kingdom."

The Jesus revealed in the Scriptures suffered unmer-
ited rejection and death. Christians cannot evade the "scandalous" fact that the One they call their Risen Lord sub-
mitted willingly to such suffering. Those who desire to be
his followers must likewise embrace suffering "for his
name's sake" on behalf of the kingdom, believing that their
suffering united to his is redemptive. Indeed, Christians
worship a God who suffers. The good news of Jesus' resur-

rection cannot remove the presence of the cross as the way of redemption from sin and death.

Conversion is the process whereby we turn to Jesus. The more deeply we encounter him the more complete will be our transformation, until someday we may be able to say with St. Paul, "Now I live, yet not I, but Christ lives in me." There is a great paradox in conversion. The Christian community encourages human formation in order that transformation will be intelligible and desirable. But when it occurs transformation often follows in the wake of the breakdown of formation. When it is recognized how inadequate our own resources are for coming to God, we are opened to God's coming to us. However conversion may occur, there are certain marks of its genuineness. Conversion plants in us the desire to know Jesus more fully, to gather together with others in a community of support for what is happening to the self, and to bear the love of Jesus which we have experienced to the world.

Living the fullness of the Christian life means striving for a life of more faithful discipleship. That will require us to leave the comfortable and familiar and to venture into the world, and there to befriend the stranger. By being his disciples we grow in the holiness belonging to God. In this manner Jesus is the reference point of Christian morality and spirituality. Both depend for their fruitfulness on meditation and prayer directed to Jesus. For we are formed by faith in the One who shared our existence, and believe that we will be exalted with him by conforming to his way of life. Having begun with Jesus, we shall consider further our encounter with the God of Jesus who gives us new hearts.

2
The Spiritual Journey

Introduction

In this chapter we consider spirituality as the process of conversion that continues throughout our lives. Christian spirituality is the journey toward wholeness of life and self-transcendence in which Jesus is the key. Many may have ambivalent feelings about "spirituality" and its connotations, feeling that their own religious experiences are too few, or too fleeting, or too ambivalent to make them capable of "spiritual" development. But is not to profess belief in the God whom Jesus reveals also to profess our capacity to receive and to be transformed by that God? Are we not, as the psalmist writes, "wonderfully made" and destined to be perfected by our Creator? If we make this profession then we must acknowledge that "a spiritual life is not a sanctuary for the saintly [but] the birthright of the baptized."[1]

We have defined spirituality as the movement of the self toward God and toward wholeness through the sharing of life with others. In the following pages we will consider how the presence of God is mediated and how we may respond. Our own experiences are the medium through

32

which we are drawn more deeply toward God. Those experiences are often illumined by others' experiences of God that have been passed down the centuries to us. In Section 1 we consider the experience of the "absence" of God out of which God's presence is paradoxically manifested. In the experience of longing for what seems to be absent, even denied, God is suddenly very close. Spiritual growth resembles physical growth insofar as it happens by a power other than our own. Yet as a process of continuing conversion it requires our active assent and cooperation. We are created with the desire for God. But the possibility of encountering God appears to be greatest when we have cultivated in our lives a rhythm of receptivity to God. Section 2 considers prayer as the striving for such a rhythm. The possibilities of transformation are inexhaustible, the conversions as unique as the circumstances in which they occur. Yet we all pass through stages of life which contain their characteristic invitations to experience God more fully. Section 3 considers the critical moments in our adult development which call us to the fullness of life.

1. Waiting for God

The search for God has long been associated with desert imagery. The Hebrews wandered for forty years in the desert; Jesus spent forty days in the desert; early Christian hermits fled to the desert in search for God. Deserts were places of potential terror: beasts of prey, intense heat and thirst, horizonless loneliness. The desert is the unfamiliar *in extremis* where people have gone to experience God. It is also symbolic of a psychological stripping of self in order to be prepared for God and to acquire the self-discipline to do God's will. The experience of seeking God is described by the sixteenth century mystic St. John of the

Cross as being enveloped in darkness. In *The Dark Night of the Soul* he records how for a long time his search for God propelled him into dark terrain, there to confront his greatest fears.

A third image of seeking the experience of God and having instead the experience of abandonment that may describe contemporary religious experiences more powerfully than deserts or darkness is "the wait." For Westerners progress is marked by increased speed and efficiency. So dependent are we on progress in these terms that having to wait is often painful and even unnerving. Deserts and darkness may inspire less fear in us than the prospect of a long wait. When we are forced to wait and when waiting lengthens or becomes indefinite, we may experience powerful, negative reactions ranging from resentment and anger to a loss of confidence and depression.

These emotions are powerfully conveyed by Samuel Beckett in his play *Waiting for Godot* (1948).[2] The play is set at a deserted country crossroad, the landscape consisting of a solitary leafless tree. The play opens with its two principal characters, Vladimir and Estragon, heatedly discussing when someone they call "Godot" will arrive. Neither knows when Godot will come and each blames the other for not knowing. Vladimir and Estragon can do nothing but wait: even their suicide attempt fails. Beckett allows for no resolution of their wait.

Beckett suggests that the only worthy and meaningful response is to endure courageously and to comfort one another. As Vladimir says:

> Let us make the most of it, before it is too late! Let us represent worthily for once the foul brood to which the cruel fate consigned us! . . . We are not saints, but we have kept our appointment. (Act II)

Vladimir's and Estragon's relationship does not become one of victim-oppressor, like that of Pozzo and Lucky, a master-slave duo who come their way. Instead, their earlier impulse to abandon each other gives way to the willingness to comfort one another's affliction. They also prove capable of showing mercy to the brutish Pozzo by rescuing him from the cruel consequences of his own deeds. *Waiting for Godot* conveys powerfully the crisis that waiting provokes. While Beckett never hints that out of the pain of waiting a transcendent meaning to human existence will be disclosed, he does offer a vision of human goodness wrought by care and sympathy. There is little for which Vladimir and Estragon can wait "in joyful hope." They are not companions on a journey but inhabitants of a cold cosmos who will do what they can to provide each other with a little warmth.

Christians share the pain of waiting although theirs is a hopeful kind of waiting. Simone Weil, a contemporary of Beckett who also lived in Paris, recorded in her journal her experiences of waiting. In *Waiting for God*, published posthumously in 1951, she writes of her encounter with God which was followed by a very long wait. She describes her experience in the following passage:

> Over the infinity of space and time, the infinitely more infinite love of God comes to possess us. . . . We have the power to consent to receive him or to refuse. If we consent, God puts a little seed in us and he goes away again. From that moment God has no more to do; neither have we, except to wait. . . . It is not as easy as it seems, for the growth of the seed in us is very painful. A day comes when the soul belongs to God, when it not only consents to love but when truly and effectively it loves.[3]

Testimonies such as Weil's encourage our hopefulness that the waiting will not be in vain because the seeds of the kingdom are growing in us—when we are doing nothing but waiting. Weil experienced the great deprivation of the early 1940's in wartime France, choosing to give up the relative comfort of a teaching position to share the suffering of the urban workers of Paris. Her waiting was a time of great suffering in imitation of Jesus' passion. Her legacy is that of a woman of great spiritual attainment.

Being made to wait forces us to reevaluate our control over our lives. Learning to wait is a most difficult struggle. Waiting is the suspension of "business as usual" in order that we may reconsider our certitude and our presuppositions as well. In *Four Quartets* T.S. Eliot speaks of the discipline of waiting:

> I said to my soul, be still, and wait without hope
> For hope would be hope for the wrong thing; wait
> 　without love
> For love would be love of the wrong thing; there is yet
> 　faith
> But the faith and the love and the hope are in the
> 　waiting.
> Wait without thought, for you are not ready for
> 　thought:
> So the darkness shall be the light, and the stillness
> 　the dancing.[4]

For Eliot the pain of waiting signals the beginning of the process of transformation. In the pain is born the knowledge and acceptance of what God is doing with us and within us. In the waiting is the awareness that we are the recipients rather than the initiators of our lives and our happiness. Eliot knew that the waiting is not easy. "You must go by a way wherein there is no ecstasy" [and] "by the way of dispossession," he writes. Dark nights, deserts, and interminable waits reflect the pain of spiritual growth.

The images of the search for God are all filled with the sense of the absence of God. But unlike Beckett's characters' unrelieved frustration, Christians who wait in thirst and in darkness believe they will not be disappointed. The images are negative not because God is absent but because we are not ready for God. We may be seeking a false god, looking for security, the avoidance of pain, or a peace based on our imagined self-superiority. God is the great disturber of our paltry peace. God strips us of all falsity until we surrender ourselves. We find in Jesus the offer of peace and wholeness, but know by his cross that we do not find peace by trying to avoid the pain of the world. The experience of the love of God will at first be harrowing because it will require us to change. As God has often been imaged as fire, spiritual growth may be called a burning process in which our lives, our pain and the pain of the world are transformed.

After the destruction of the temple in Jerusalem in 587 B.C.E. and during the Israelites' exile in Babylon, the psalmist wrote

> With my whole being I thirst for God, the living God.
> When shall I come to God and appear in his
>   presence? . . .
> I call to mind how I marched in the ranks of the great
>   to the house of God. . . .
> How deep I am sunk in misery, groaning in my
>   distress:
> Yet I will wait for God (Ps 42:2, 4, 11)

Israel's experience is not simply of absence but of loss. They have known the joy of home but are now exiled and restlessly waiting for a return. As for them, waiting is imposed upon us, but it is also something we may choose in order to break out of the routine and listen for the divine presence. Then the time of waiting becomes a time of praying.

2. Teach Us To Pray

Prayer is the suspension of time and the adoption of a patient and quiet heart in order that we might be led into deeper communion with God. Praying requires stepping out of the current of activities in which we are caught up. Jesus' interruption of his preaching and healing is paradigmatic of the role of prayer in the Christian life. Mark writes of Jesus that "long before dawn, he got up and left the house and went off to a lonely place and prayed there" (Mk 1:35). Henri Nouwen says of this passage:

> The more I read this nearly silent sentence locked in between the loud words of action, the more I have the sense that the secret of Jesus' ministry is hidden in that lonely place where he went to pray, early in the morning, long before dawn.[5]

Amidst all of the action is the need to withdraw into quietude.

The intense level of activity and distractions in life often fills up every available moment. Anxious and driven, we have no vacancy of heart or mind for any reality beyond immediate self-need. Prayer is first of all the intention to create an opening, a space where we might wait for the stirrings of God. Prayer, in whatever form it takes, calls us to deeper receptivity. What we will most likely experience first is not God speaking to us but the swirl of our own anxieties seeking our attention. Praying is attempting to stand in all humility before a liberating presence in which we can be sufficiently freed from what makes us anxious in order to listen and respond.

Let us briefly consider three modes of prayer: verbal prayer, meditative prayer focused on the Scriptures, and contemplative prayer. Since God is the giver of all intimations of himself these three varieties of prayer ought not to be seen as dependent on human work or as corresponding to a progressive movement from "beginner" to "virtuoso." We are all beginners at prayer.

Jesus' disciples asked him to teach them how to pray. The prayer he taught them—"our Father in heaven, may your name be held holy . . ."—is a prayer of trust in the Father and of hope in the coming of the kingdom. Verbal prayer, communal and individual, reminds us of the gratitude and obedience we owe God. In the rhythms of words we express our filial relationship to God, pledging ourselves to doing the Father's will "on earth as in heaven" and acknowledging our neediness.

A second mode of prayer was known by medieval Christians as *lectio divina*, or "sacred reading." It begins with the reading of the words of Scripture in order that they will penetrate our understandings as well as our affective life. Thomas Keating describes the process:

> Each period of *lectio divina* follows the same plan: reflection on the Word of God, followed by free expression of the spontaneous feelings that arise in our hearts. The whole gamut of human response to truth, beauty, goodness, and love is possible. As the heart reaches out in longing for God, it begins to penetrate the words of the sacred text.[6]

In more colloquial terms Keating compares the practice of *lectio divina* to being in the presence of another in order that a friendship might develop.

The knowledge mediated by the Scriptures is not only informative but formative and transformative. At times the Christian community has not recognized the power of the Scriptures as prayer. For example, St. Teresa of Avila recorded in her autobiography that she often sought God by meditation on Jesus' "sacred humanity" and his passion by reading from the Scriptures, even though the theologians of her day discouraged such exercise of the imagination.[7] Teresa reported no extraordinary encounters with Jesus but spoke of feeling his presence, contemplating his agony in the garden, and being moved to great sorrow for his suffering and resolving to do his will. Another spiritual seeker of the time, St. Ignatius, inspired a method of prayer that relied on a meditative and imaginative approach to reading Scripture. Teresa and Ignatius remind us that Scripture is not an historical record but a place of intersection between the human and divine. For as Keating writes, in the course of meditation on the Scriptures the Holy Spirit explains their meaning to us in order that they may serve as "a means of communing with God."[8]

A third mode of prayer is experienced without the use of words or texts. While Jesus' prayers are recorded in several places in the Gospels, oftentimes it is only stated that he went off to a lonely place. The silence of the text reflects the silence of such prayer itself. In those silences comes the fuller discernment of the will of God for each of us. Variously described as "prayer of quiet" and "prayer of the heart," this kind of prayer involves being led by Jesus deeper into the mystery of God. In *The Way of a Pilgrim*, a seventeenth century book of Eastern Orthodox spirituality, the master speaks of a state of prayer in which one "catches sight . . . of some of the mysteries of the Kingdom of God." To experience such prayer, he continues, requires only that we make "the effort to sink down in silence into the depths of one's heart and call more and more on the radiant name of Jesus."[9]

The goal of all of these ways of prayer is to experience more deeply the love of God. The final fruit of prayer is what God reveals to the waiting and listening heart. The self is relinquished to be "played upon" as the instrument of divine love. Simone Weil describes what she felt in this way:

> A day comes when the soul belongs to God. . . . The love within is divine, uncreated; for it is the love of God for God that is passing through it. We can only consent to give up our feelings so as to allow free passage in our soul for this love.[10]

The "giving up" she refers to leads to wholeness and unsurpassable peace.

This sort of experience is often associated with contemplative prayer. Contemplation is a divine gift experienced as powerful love. Merton is suggesting a contemplative experience when he speaks of God's love as "a great wave washing us, gathering us in, in order to bring us back to Him on the tide of his infinite mercy."[11] The image of being carried away may be as harrowing as it is consoling; indeed, friendship with God means acknowledging God's control over our lives. Yet it is in just such loss that we gain knowledge of our true identity.

Contemplation is a rare kind of prayer experience. Yet Merton claims that it is given to "those who ask the question what is the will of God for me and who live its honest answer."[12] Communion with God and discernment of God's will are inseparable aspects of prayer. As such, they remind us of the real connection between the contemplative and active dimensions of the Christian life.

St. Teresa's description of her own life of prayer offers valuable insight into the life of prayer. She describes her efforts at prayer throughout the course of many years by comparing them to the variety of ways in which one might water a garden.[13] The first efforts at prayer she likens to watering the garden by drawing water from a well. Much effort is required for only a little water. More advanced efforts, such as longer periods of meditation, she compares to the use of a waterwheel. Here, a good deal more water is produced but still constant effort is required. A third source of water involves opening a channel fed by a river to produce a great flow of water with little effort. Finally, the garden will be watered bountifully and effortlessly simply by the rain. The less complicated and laborious her prayer became, the greater was the inflowing of God's presence into her spirit. Teresa makes it clear that only after many years did her prayer become effortless and that, even then, she often needed to go back to the well, as it were.

Also associated with prayer is the practice traditionally known as "mortification." While formal penitential practices have been deemphasized in post-Vatican II Catholicism, the Church continues to recognize the importance of self-mortification in Christian life. But mortification is often understood as a punishment we impose on ourselves for delighting in the world too much. Such a conception of mortification seems to suggest that spiritual progress only happens by turning away from the world rather than delighting in it. Mortification, as the word suggests, is related to death, not in the negative ways of denying the creation, but in dying to that part of ourselves which refuses to accept diminishment and death. The pain of mortification is not arbitrarily chosen or imposed. Rather, mortification is willingness to share in the pain of the world and to recognize that often we are the cause of the suffering of others. We need not seek out suffering: pain is plentifully present all around us, if we can only see it. Our tendency is not to confront it but to maintain the fiction that it is not really there—or not really ours. Mortification is entry into the world's pain and begins with recognizing the most proximate forms which we cause by commission and omission.

The pain around us is an invitation to come to terms with ourselves, to die to certain images of ourselves and patterns of thought and action which produce suffering for self and others. Mortification may mean confronting our own failures to live with and serve others. It is shedding old habits and masks by which we have played false and failed to love. It is dying to that self which has not acknowledged neediness for others and absolute need for God. Genuine mortification is also found in sharing the pain and suffering of others. When we identify with the oppression others experience we see that their suffering is also ours. Truly, care for them means acknowledging that the possibility of their healing is also the possibility of our own healing.

Mortification can also mean seeking meaning in the suffering which is part of our human condition. Perhaps this is what Flannery O'Connor was hinting at in remarking that an acquaintance of hers "did not know what to do with his suffering." Genuine mortification does not deny the world or seek escape from it. Rather, through it we are purified for fuller openness to God and to one another.

3. Human Development as Spiritual Growth

Waiting is an orientation toward the future, toward what is yet to happen. But anticipation of the future must not cause us to miss the present possibilities for transformation. St. Paul exhorts the Corinthians, "Now is the favorable time; this is the day of salvation" (2 Cor 6:2). The kingdom

Jesus proclaimed will be fully revealed in the future but has begun with him. The divine intent is being fulfilled now. The following paragraphs consider the significance of the present moment for spiritual growth, looking especially at the phases of the adult life process.

Erik Erikson describes three crisis periods of adult psychological development, each associated with a span of years demarcating young, middle, and later adulthood. By "crisis" Erikson does not mean an event that is single, sudden or dramatic—although some might experience a crisis this way—but psychologically challenging occasions which, if successfully surmounted, increase our capacity for further life and growth. Erikson speaks of the "vital personality" weathering such crises and reemerging "with increased powers of self-understanding and action."[14]

Our consideration of adult psychological development through the resolution of these crises is not intended to suggest that these are the exclusive times and occasions in which spiritual growth occurs. Yet developmental crises have in common with other life crises that they require us to reassess who we are and what we should be doing. Vilma Seelaus notes that "crisis times are more than challenges to psychological growth. They are stirrings of awareness of divine centeredness and deeper entry into God-us relatedness."[15] The crises we shall discuss each requires a kind of dying to certain expectations and self-images and a rising to more truthful ones. Crises may occur suddenly and traumatically or they may be protracted and only moderately painful. In whatever form they are experienced, crises challenge us to develop new traits and skills in order that we may modify particular patterns of behavior.

The crisis of early adulthood occurs in conjunction with the establishment of psychological independence which marks the beginning of adulthood. The achievement of a separate identity and of self-reliance begins to reveal another need, the need for intimacy. Separateness must be complemented by a sharing of self with others. Erikson notes several psychological capacities which must be acquired in order to resolve the "crisis of intimacy": attentiveness and empathy toward others, a flexible sense of self that allows for change on the basis of what others tell us about ourselves, and the resiliency to be changed without loss of self. Erikson describes the variety of contexts in which mutuality and intimacy are learned, ranging from romantic relationships to family relationships and to group activity, that are collaborative or competitive.

A central theme to be developed in this book (and most explicitly in the final chapter) is that friendship with God and with others is the goal of the Christian life. Spirituality and morality both aim at such attainment. Friendship and intimacy are achieved by breaking out of our limited self-awareness and finding fuller life by sharing life. True friendship recognizes our need to give and receive support from each other. In short, it is friendship that reminds us that we are made for each other's company. Learning intimacy is the antidote to our negative tendencies to draw back from others in suspicion or to impose our self-images on the rest of reality, closing ourselves off from the ultimate reality in which we live and move and have our being. We have spoken of prayer as friendship with God. We should also observe how difficult it is to be intimate with God if we cannot attain community and shared life with human beings. Indeed, friendship is a fundamental need and the way into the presence of God.

In addition to the capacity for intimacy is the challenge to commit the self to the service of others. Erikson describes this as the "crisis of care" in which a balance must be achieved between furthering one's own needs and making sacrifices on behalf of others. The need in the middle of life is to commit the self to something of enduring worth, and to sacrifice the self in substantial ways for it. As intimacy means recognizing our need to be with others, caring means developing and sustaining various ways of living for others. Erikson calls the critical achievement at this stage of life "generativity." Life is increased and enhanced through parenting and many other forms of active caring for others.

We have already noted that the test of the genuineness of conversion is whether it draws us forth to the active love of others. Spiritual growth is also simultaneous extension of the range of our care. Self-centeredness is a false consciousness which saps the energy necessary for a life of care, while the discovery of authentic self ("transformation") gives us new energy for loving others. Haughton's description of a life crisis which leads to conversion illustrates the "crisis of care." Recall that in her account the man has never been more than lukewarm either to his family or to a wider community. He has made an effort at engagement by joining a political activist community but this initiative has not rescued him from the crisis. The emptiness of his life becomes increasingly unbearable and a breakdown occurs. His transformation occurs only when in his deepest anguish he suddenly discovers he is loved and cared about and finds the strength with which to care for others. While Erikson treats generativity as a "normal" adult achievement, Haughton describes it as an achievement of grace, namely, as one of the variety of ways in which God provides us with the experience of the power of divine love through our own adult journeys.

A third stage Erikson identifies is associated with later life. The critical need now is to understand as best one can the course which one's life has taken and to accept the self.

Erikson calls this simply the "crisis of wisdom." It is not that life is now over or that a summit has been reached from which to look back. One is still in the middle of things. While circumstances and health slow one's pace, there is new leisure for learning and much yet to learn. Meeting the challenge of wisdom will be assisted by the habits of self-inquiry one has learned earlier in life. Conversely, it is unlikely that people who never could bear to wait will find the waiting in later life to be bearable.

We may still learn lessons in later life which we failed to learn earlier. New enthusiasm for life may be kindled by the recognition that one's time is short. An octogenarian writes of her later life experiences:

> My seventies were interesting and fairly serene, but my eighties are passionate. I grow more intense as I age. To my surprise I burst out with hot convictions. Now I am so disturbed by the outer world and by human quality in general that I want to put things right as though I still owed a debt to life.[16]

The elderly who occupy the majority of the church pews are not there, I suspect, because of their fear of dying and the need to make amends. Indeed, they may be aware of past failures. But their presence may reflect in fact that they have learned how to wait, how to "waste time" in prayer, how to befriend and spend themselves for others. If they have learned these things, they have journeyed far and feel close to home. Like St. Paul they may indeed wish to be with God.

We have discussed three stages in adult life. Each involves a "crisis" which may be felt with varying intensity. Crisis times may be marked by the feeling that one has lost the ability to cope. Such vulnerability is the occasion for enduring personal growth if the crisis is successfully surmounted. These crises are the times in which salvation is being offered to us. The new powers we acquire as a result of these crises give us the ability to continue our spiritual journey. In *Christian Life Patterns*, Evelyn and James Whitehead call the critical skills Erikson describes both "the indispensable components of effective behavior" and "the stuff of Christian asceticism."[17] They remind us that holiness is not to be "equated either with childhood, metaphorical or real, or with perfect and final maturity."[18] Instead it is offered to us in the dynamic life process, and especially in times of crisis.

4. One Spirit, One Body

In the Introduction we noted how a two-tier conception of the Christian life has created a gulf between religious and lay vocations and between Christian spirituality and morality. The functional division of Christianity into religious and laity ends up detracting from both ways of life by obscuring what is common to both. Consider how many people view the vocation of vowed religious people. Life in religious community may seem strange (and the monastic way of life the strangest of all). Why, many may ask, would anyone choose the life of a monk or a contemplative nun? What purpose does such a reclusive existence serve? Even people familiar with monasteries and appreciative of the dedication of those in "religious life" may still misunderstand the relationship between monastic life and the lives of Christians living "in the world."

"Religious life" in this narrow sense refers to the state of life to which relatively few are called. Full commitment to it is reflected in lives of poverty, chastity, and obedience. Monasteries and religious communities are not separated from the rest by their holiness. Monks, nuns, and other vowed religious are like other Christians and experience both success and failure in their aspirations as do the rest of us. Because all are called to experience the presence of God, to be given new hearts and to be made holy, we must recognize that the difference between lay Christians and vowed religious is a difference in the route chosen rather than in the destination to which all are called. Granted, the insights of St. Teresa of Avila and contemporary monks like Thomas Merton and Thomas Keating are most helpful in the spiritual journeys of religious and lay people alike. But those who have not taken religious vows may often miss the central message of these people. We are not two classes of Christians—spiritual olympians and pedestrians, as it were—but a community of Christians seeking God by different paths.

Our own spiritual journeys can be assisted by overcoming the attitude which says, in effect, "I don't live in a monastery and cannot cultivate the daily rhythm of prayer which real spiritual advancement would require." Those who live in religious communities are the first to dispel any "class distinction" between themselves and those outside the walls. They acknowledge that religious life has its own perils and temptations, and is far from free of distractions and turmoil, and is a constant challenge in the development of loving relationships among its members. Merton has answered the question of whether the vowed religious life is a privileged place for learning to pray and for becoming holy with a firm "No." The vocation of monks, he says, is to make prayer their explicit daily work.

The view that there are two classes of Christians persists. Yet everything we have spoken of here—the waiting that life imposes on us, the cultivation of prayer, and the critical passages of life—is a part of every life. The spiritual life is every Christian's birthright. While action and contem-

plation describe different "moments" or phases of our lives,
it is never accurate to describe the Christian vocation strictly
in terms of one or the other. Contemplation and action are
integral elements of the Christian life. As monks must care
deeply about the shape God's world is in and how God's
children are being treated, so every Christian living in the
world is called "to build his or her own kind of enclosure as
far as one's duties allow, by setting aside a certain amount
of time every day for prayer and spiritual reading."[19] We
build our own enclosures for prayer when we recognize that
we are called to holiness. Every way of life and every kind of
work is in need of such enclosures.

On the day of his death Thomas Merton was addressing a group of Christian monks in Thailand who had
gathered to consider the future of monasticism and to meet
with their Buddhist counterparts. "From now on," Merton
observed, "everybody stands on his own feet."[20] What did
he mean? He quickly made it clear that he did not mean we
could go on without the power of God's grace. Nor did he
mean, I suspect, that Christians—either those under religious vows or lay people—had to "go it alone" in their
religious journeys without the encouragement and assist-
ance of the Christian churches. Rather, what he seemed to
mean was that today's Christians cannot depend on a
Christian cultural structure to promote experiences of God.
Karl Rahner seemed to be making the same point when he
said that in the future all Christians must be "mystics" in
quest of their own experience of God rather than expecting
a "second-hand" religious experience from living in the
midst of a religious culture. We must "stand on our own
feet" because our culture less and less points us toward
the sacred.

But more is required of us than desiring the experience
of God. Where and how we seek God is crucial. While

Merton found monastic discipline a valuable aid he did not see the monastery as itself conferring holiness on its inhabitants. He often reminded his fellow monks that they could not hide out in the monastery. What holiness monastic communities have depends on their loving service to others. By communion with others—which begins with the affirmation that all others are our neighbors—we shall discover the One who inhabits all persons and renders them holy ground. In such a way of living the Spirit will nourish us, enabling us to bear in our lives the fruits of "patience, kindness, goodness, trustfulness, gentleness and self-control" (Gal 5:23). The way to God is not a journey out of the world; instead, it is an imitation of the ways of God as St. Paul describes them. Working for the healing of the world's brokenness shall yield the unexpected joy of reconciliation with God.

Conclusion

We have attempted to describe the movement toward God in the experiences of waiting, in embarking on various pathways of prayer, and in discerning the presence of God in certain critical periods of life. Corresponding to a deepened experience of God is greater capacity for life with others. Knowing ourselves, acknowledging that we belong to God and with others—these are, as we noted at the outset, the integrated spiritual and moral tasks of Christians. In the next three chapters we will examine the nature of the moral life to which Christians as Jesus' disciples are being called. As we look at the moral issues we face, the temptation to violence, the faces of sin, and the power of God's grace to foster virtue in us, we hope to make it more evident that in all of these "moral" matters our transformation to fuller life with God and one another is at stake.

3
The Christian Moral Life

Introduction

Our approach to the Christian moral life is to view it as intimately connected with and the fruit of the process of ongoing conversion and self-transcendence that goes by the name of Christian spirituality. In the Introduction we noted the central moral imperative of the Gospels is to love one another. We also suggested that loving is so difficult precisely because of the fear and anxiety that are the consequence of not knowing ourselves in our essential relatedness to God. In the first chapter we considered Jesus as the compassionate presence of God who will teach us how to love. We are called to imitate his prayerful orientation toward the Father and his single-hearted desire to do the Father's will. Christians believe that by conversion, by "putting on Christ," they receive the power to love their neighbor. Conversion and discipleship have as their consequences the capacity for ever more effective loving.

What we will say about the Christian moral life has as its context the efforts underway in Roman Catholicism to renew its theology of the moral life. The Second Vatican

Council gave official recognition and impetus to renewal efforts going on within the Catholic Church. Among those efforts was the desire to reinvigorate Catholic perceptions of morality by more closely linking it to the life of faith. Toward that end the Council urged that moral theology be "renewed by livelier contact with the mystery of Christ and the history of salvation," that it be "more thoroughly nourished by scriptural teaching," and that it stress the "nobility of the Christian vocation of the faithful and their obligation to bring forth fruit in charity for the life of the world."[1]

The need for the renewal of Catholic moral theology resulted from a two-century-old trend in which moral teaching was cut off from its theological source. The moral theology of the nineteenth century manualists, for example, bore little resemblance to the *Summa* which Thomas Aquinas had produced in the thirteenth century interweaving dogmatic, moral, and spiritual theology into a unified examination of the Christian life. A recent commentator writes of the organization of the *Summa* that in its first part Aquinas considers human beings as "wholly from God" and in the second part considers them as "wholly to God," while the third and final part considers Jesus Christ as the incomparable link between God and humanity.[2] Aquinas' account of the moral life (Part Two), examining the human response to God's self-revelation (Part One), never loses sight of the fact that human happiness depends upon receptivity to God and that human fulfillment is achieved finally in union with God. After Thomas, so-called "summas" limited to morality began to appear. In the nineteenth century, moral manuals were produced for the purpose of preparing priests to hear confessions. Such manuals had little to say about the connection between the Christian moral life as response to and deepening of conversion. Instead, the moral life was presented as a matter of conforming one's conduct to the dictates of natural law—that is, the eternal law as it can be known to human reason. In such an emphasis God becomes more the remote source of cosmic order to which we must conform than the one who calls us to the fullness of life through Jesus Christ.

As we have noted, the moral renewal has begun but is far from completed. Many Catholics are not inspired by their Church's moral teachings to see their moral lives as the bearing of fruits of faith, in large part because of three centuries of separating moral practice from conversion process. One of the paths which renewal is only beginning to take is that of reforging the link between morality and spirituality. For Christian spirituality is the invitation to a more Christ-centered way of life that has charity as its practical commitment. Without spirituality the moral life would be misperceived. By emphasizing the link between the spiritual and moral dimensions of the Christian life, this account hopes to contribute to that renewal process.

This chapter will offer an account of the Christian moral life. In the first section we will describe the central orientation of Christian morality that lends it distinctiveness. We will look at three different ways in which the Christian tradition has attempted to describe the moral orientation which flows from Christian faith. The second section focuses on the nature of moral agency, leaving to the fifth chapter an examination of the particular character traits which Christians are encouraged to develop. Section three examines some of the ways in which the very concept of morality is deformed nowadays. By recognizing why such views reflect mistaken attitudes about our relationship with God, Christians are better able to understand what is distinctive about their moral life.

1. Three Models of the Moral Life

Christian morality is grounded on the conviction that God is calling us to be a community which endeavors to respond to what God is doing and so to imitate God. Here we will consider three ways in which Christians have described what Christian morality is about. The first and second approaches are of ancient origin, the first issuing from ancient Israel and the second from Aristotle. The third approach has been articulated recently by American Protestant ethicist, H. Richard Niebuhr. Each of these models has a particular emphasis; however, they are not to be construed as mutually exclusive. While deficiencies of the first and second models will be noted and Niebuhr's model given greatest attention, none of these models will be dismissed.

In the ancient Israelite account the moral life was perceived as abiding by the precepts which Yahweh had established through the act of creation and of making the covenant with Israel. Morality first of all entails conforming to the norms, both obligations and prohibitions, which God has ordained. The "holiness codes" of ancient Israel (such as found in Leviticus 19:2: "You shall be holy: for I the Lord your God am holy") make clear that the law was not merely intended to avoid the wrath of God but to draw human beings into the divine presence. Morality as obedience to the law came to dominate the ethos of both Jews and Christians. In Jesus' teaching the law is not repudiated but deepened. Jesus tells his hearers that the law was given to Moses for their edification. Indeed, the law was given to Israel as a guide and a means of becoming a holy people.

The second approach fastens not on law but on the notion of the final end or ultimate good which is to be realized through the moral life. Central to Aristotle's ethics was his emphasis on the attainment of wisdom as the end or the *telos* of practical and speculative activity. Aquinas adapted Aristotle to Christian belief by positing as the goal of all human activity the attainment of the vision of God. In their analysis of the moral life both Aristotle and Aquinas paid attention to the virtues one needed to perfect to live a well-ordered life and reach one's proper end.

The models of obedience to the laws of God or attainment of the vision of God both offer us a partial understanding of the Christian moral life. But neither captures the sense of morality as the call to imitate the life and likeness of God. The end vision model has its shortcomings. It might suggest that we can know ahead of time the end toward which we are moving, when in fact we only come to know God in the journey. It looks to the future, perhaps at some expense to the present. It suggests a rather orderly progression to a future already known. The obedience model has shortcomings which we will address later in this chapter.

Having suggested the limitations of both the "end vision" and "obedience-to-law" models of the Christian moral life, Niebuhr offered another way of describing the moral life. His vision of the moral life began with the conviction that as moral subjects we are more acted upon than acting. Niebuhr viewed moral agency as essentially given to responding to or answering what is being done and said to us. He wrote:

> What is implicit in the idea of responsibility is the image man-the-answerer, man engaged in dialogue, man acting in response to action upon him. . . . To be engaged in dialogue, to answer questions addressed to us, to defend ourselves against attacks, to reply to injunctions, to meet challenges—this is common experience. And

now we try to think of all our actions as having this character of being responses, answers, to actions upon us.[3]

Niebuhr saw the Christian life in terms of ever-deepening discernment of and attunement with the movements of the One who is Creator, Redeemer and Sustainer. Our first task, Niebuhr claimed, is neither to obey the law nor to seek our final end but to respond in a fitting way to what is being said and done to us by others and by the divine "Other." Most of what we call "doing" is actually a matter of "responding" to what is happening to us.

For Niebuhr ethics was foremost an interpretive activity. What makes our actions responses rather than merely reactions is the interpretation that accompanies them. It is this reflective phase that makes them "moral" actions. As Niebuhr put it, ethical inquiry begins when we are prompted to ask "What is going on?"[4] As we interpret what is happening and how we are being acted upon, a second question presses upon us: How ought we to respond to what is happening? All of moral inquiry, whether about the "rightness" of action or of the "goodness" of our lives, arises in the swirl of forces and persons acting upon us. We desire to know where we stand in order to respond in a "fitting" way—literally, in a manner that fits into the rhythm of ultimate reality.[5] This is the interpretive activity underlying the formal moral questions "What should I do?" and "Is it morally right to . . . ?"

Niebuhr's articulation of the response nature of the moral life broadens our understanding of Christian ethics. His central observations, that we are being acted upon prior to our own acting and that we need to bring all our powers of discernment to determining what we ought to be doing, moves ethical reflection in the direction of Christian spirituality. For in the awareness that we are being acted upon by powers beyond our ability to control and that our task is to respond comes a new sense of moral agency. We begin to fathom the presence of a power that is above, beneath, around, and at the essence of the moral self who lives and acts. We necessarily become prayerful people—or are at least encouraged to become so. Niebuhr's emphasis upon interpretation included not only cognitive activity but also the powers of intuition, imagination, feeling, and memory, the very affective ways of knowing that prayer encourages.

Christian morality has been informed by a particular story of divine action and human response. The story is that of Israel and of Jesus of Nazareth. The story of Jesus is that of a single-minded journey to God. The scriptural stories serve to illuminate the way for the rest of us, in order that we might someday share in divine life. Niebuhr put large emphasis on the scriptural stories as the revelation of God's saving deeds. He also suggested our essentially interpretive response to them.

> At the critical junctures of the history of Israel and of the early Christian community the decisive question men raised was not "What is the goal?" nor yet "What is the law?" but "What is happening?" and then "What is the fitting response to what is happening?" . . . The God to whom Jesus points is not the commander who gives laws but the doer of small and of mighty deeds, the creator of sparrows and clother of lilies, the ultimate giver of blindness and of sight, the ruler whose rule is hidden in the manifold activities of plural agencies but is yet in a way visible to those who know how to inter-pret the signs of the times.[6]

While Niebuhr did not speak of the self-images arising from the stories that individuals and communities tell about themselves, others who have been influenced by his stress on interpretation have explored the role of "narrative" or "story" in helping to reveal images of the self. They have suggested how important the stories we tell are for imaging and reimaging the self in relation to all else. Through interpretation of the Scriptures we hope to be able to respond more fittingly to what God has done and is doing and so to form more truthful images of ourselves.

Niebuhr's understanding of the moral life highlights the divine activity in the world and the human activity that is meant to be a fitting response to the many ways in which we are acted upon. In the next section we will look more closely at how Christianity is to understand moral agency.

2. Moral Agency as Response to Holiness

Nowhere in the New Testament is there a fuller description of the "ethic of the kingdom" than in the Sermon on the Mount (Mt 5-7; Lk 6). There Jesus urges his hearers to be compassionate, to love one's enemies, to forgive, to be peacemakers—in short, to be transformed by trusting in the goodness of the Father. Jesus' teaching moves from the letter of the law to its spirit (e.g., "You have heard that it was said to the men of old, 'You shall not kill. . . .' But I say to you that whoever insults his brother shall be liable . . . "—Mt 5:21-22). He summarizes what he has in mind by saying simply "You, therefore, must be perfect, as your heavenly Father is perfect" (Mt 5:48). The Sermon on the Mount, with its climactic call to perfection, raises serious questions. Is this body of teaching to be interpreted eschatologically, referring to a way of life to be anticipated when the kingdom of God is fully realized? Indeed, the perfection to which human beings are called involves a completion which cannot be either fully known or attained in the present.

Nonetheless, it is not warranted to interpret what Jesus taught as a future reality present now only as an ideal. The call to perfection after the manner of God's perfection is a call to present movement toward the fullness of life.

Jesus' call to "be perfect" recalls the Holiness Code of ancient Israel, in which the purpose of observing the law is summarized repeatedly in the refrain "You shall be holy, for I the Lord your God am holy" (Lev 19:2). If indeed perfection and holiness take us to the heart of the Christian moral life, what do they require of us? To be perfect cannot mean to become God, since God is, was, and will be "other" than we are. Yet the divine attribute of holiness is not meant to inspire such awe and fear that we dare not approach God. Human perfection and holiness must mean in some way the penetration of divine reality into ours. Merton located the attainment of holiness in the desire "to offer to God the worship of our imitation."[7] To become like God is to imitate the ways of God by discerning and following God's will. Holiness is both a matter of doing God's will and of knowing who we are. "The problem of sanctity and salvation," Merton said, "is in fact the problem of finding out who I am and of discovering my true self."[8] Merton reflected on human holiness:

> Trees and animals have no problem. God makes them what they are without consulting them, and they are perfectly satisfied. With us it is different. God leaves us free to be whatever we like. We can be ourselves or not, as we please. But the problem is this: *since God alone possesses the secret of my identity, He alone can make me who I am* or, rather, He alone can make me who I will be when I at last fully begin to be.
>
> *The seeds that are planted in my liberty at every moment are the seeds of my own identity, my own reality, my own happiness, my own sanctity.*[9]

Both the models of attaining the vision of God and of obedience to the will of God have holiness as the ultimate moral purpose of humankind. But Niebuhr's model of response puts most emphasis on human action as the constant attempt to know who we are and to whom we belong. For Niebuhr, the Christian moral life is a process of ever greater discernment of God in our encounter with self and with others. When Christian morality is seen as transformation to holiness, I believe we can more readily see our everyday lives as spiritual journeys. The remainder of this section will reflect on how we might use our moral capacities of will, reason, and freedom toward greater knowledge of self and the worship of God which is our imitation of God's ways.

As Niebuhr reminded us, our moral activity is primarily response to what others and the divine Other are doing to us. Here we will consider the faculties of moral response. In ethical analysis persons are often referred to as "moral agents" in order to emphasize that they are engaged in making moral decisions. The term is not a particularly happy one. No one refers to herself or himself as a "moral agent"; besides, the term misleadingly suggests a turning on and off or a compartmentalizing of life activities (now I am playing a moral role, making moral judgments, etc.) that is not true. Aquinas employed no such term. His discussions of moral action, including the process of human intentionality and will, reason and freedom, the notion of virtue and the particular virtues, and the fact of sin are integrated into his discussion of how human beings are acted upon. Here he considers the actions upon us as God's grace manifested in the variety of charisms, in prophetic activity, and in contemplation. Let us consider how Aquinas described human moral faculties and the effects of sin upon them.

As we noted in the first section, the context of all

human activity is our personal relatedness to God. Aquinas describes human acts as voluntary because they have as their "internal principle" human agents; at the same time agents and their acts have God as their "first principle."[10] Aquinas' discussion of human acts is linked to his discussion of happiness ("Since we cannot come to happiness save through some activity we now have to attend to human acts, so that we may learn which of them will open the way and which of them will block it").[11] He defines human acts as those which depend upon interaction of the reason and the will,[12] the latter which he describes as "the rational appetite proper to human beings."[13] Thomas also noted the effect of sin in upsetting the operation of reason and will. Although the will is "rationally controlled," the effect of sin is to make it less rational. Our reasoning process is weakened and our wills weakened even more.

Sin debilitates our capacity for making a fitting response. We now see the world as through a "fisheye" lens in which the "I" dominates and distorts the horizon. Our desire for just and loving relations with others often gives way to the desire to defend the self against others. "Rationalization" is reason excessively under the influence of self-interest. As a result of the corruption of our moral faculties we find ourselves in a radically fragmented world.

The effects of sin are plainly evident in our own cultural understanding of freedom. The notion of freedom as unimpeded personal advancement and self-indulgence has proved to be enslaving. Freedom as the right "to do anything I choose to do as long as nobody gets hurt" has produced a society offering little support to its members, and least of all to its disadvantaged members. The remedy being offered nowadays to excessive claims of freedom, that freedom be balanced with recognition of responsibility, is not adequate to the disease. For renunciation of sin and recovery of true freedom mean resisting the pride and selfishness which is part of who we are. Hauerwas notes that all accounts of freedom that exalt "our neurotic self-preoccupation" are false because they prevent us from seeing the world as it really is.[14] He defines freedom as "the disciplined overcoming of the self that allows for the clarification of our vision; to be free is to exist sanely without fear, to perceive what is real."[15] Being free means finally being able to affirm the separateness of others that allows us to be freed *for* relationship with them.

It may be useful to consider human moral faculties and the call to holiness by exploring the distinction between the human capacity for intentional activity and for attentiveness. In adulthood we are continually faced with the need to relearn the attentiveness to the world which children often exhibit. For adults become more intentive, pursuing goals, working at specialized occupations through which we hope to achieve self-realization. Intentionality, as the capacity for deliberative activity, is not undesirable. Indeed, adults must be able to establish goals and develop the means to attain them. Psychologist Rollo May describes loving and willing as intentional activities essential to well-being. In the absence of such capacities people suffer from the profound effects of apathy. On the other hand, it is often the case that we suffer from a tyranny of intention, in which we plunge ahead with little sense of what we are seeking.

Attentiveness is the process of training the self to be receptive to the world and to others. Henri Nouwen writes that the ability to care for others is diminished by the inability to be "present" to them in the sense of discovering their own reality rather than imposing ourselves upon them—even with "good intentions."[16] Attentiveness is necessary to find the true self often lost in the pursuits of the ego. Much of what passes for virtuoso performances of self-made men and women misses what attentiveness has to teach: life is a gift that is only fully lived through receptivity to the reality around us.

Attentiveness is a constitutive part of the moral life. It is a moral skill. Corruption of our reason and our will results in desires unrestrained by disciplined attentiveness to the world. Hauerwas reminds us of the necessity of attentiveness, observing:

> The moral life is more a matter of attention than it is of will; one becomes good by training attentiveness to recognize the loved object with equality and fairness. For the lover is constantly tempted to see himself as being either above or below the object of his love, and this can only result in a master-slave relationship. Attentiveness is that aspect of our moral life which enables us to love the other as an equal through the accurate apprehension of his reality.[17]

Out of the capacity for attentiveness to the world grows an appreciation for its beauty, immensity and mystery. Being attentive to other realities so that we may be truly appreciative of them is the basis of attraction and communion between persons.

Human purposes are more than sequences of tasks to be completed. When we are driven by the need to accomplish tasks, we often lose sight of the reasons for which we are doing them. Seeking answers to the question of the meaning and purpose of our lives entails close attention to the world around us. It is often the work we do when there is nothing occupying us and we have no task to complete. For it is by means of both attentiveness and intentional activity that we move toward fullness of life. Attentiveness is necessary to develop the reflective dimension of life.

Accounts of moral agency often put heavy stress on making choices and decisions but too little stress on the imagination we need to understand ourselves rightly in the complexity and flux of the world. In offering his account of the moral agent as "responder," Niebuhr sought to emphasize the necessity of attentiveness. Moral growth resembles artistic capacity in a significant way: both depend upon becoming attentive to the world in its endless variety.

I have avoided talking about achieving holiness or living the moral life as human "tasks" because of the connotations of that word. We spend most of our lives completing tasks one after another—some carried out almost unconsciously, others pursued quite purposefully. Eventually, we come to view our fulfillment as the successful completion of all the tasks stretching out ahead of us. The so-called "productive" years mark our most strenuous dedication to such tasks. But human fulfillment does not come through the completion of any number of tasks. And human fulfillment specified in terms of transformation to holiness most certainly does not. Our lives are a process of the continuous unfolding of experience in which past and future are united in the present. As Christians, we most aptly talk about life as a process of submitting ourselves to God's leading. We are being led toward the Holy One by way of the community that has sought historically to be a holy people. This way of talking about the moral life may be an aid to our self-perception insofar as it moves the focus away from the "task" character of life (especially in the Western world) and toward thinking about the skills and disciplines we will need to make the journey. As I shall note below, the awareness that we are submitting to a process may help us to resist the tendency to see our life projects as improving self and world.

We are not the agents of our transformation to holi-

ness. This is not to say that we can do nothing to assist the
process. The control we possess is of a paradoxical sort: it is
the control of knowing when and how to let go, which is
best captured in Jesus' words: "Anyone who loses his life
for my sake will find it" (Mt 16:25). Indeed, we must be
watching out for the opportunities and occasions for transformation in order to avail ourselves of them.

3. The Corruption and Chastening of Ethics

We began this chapter by claiming that Christianity
possesses an alternative vision of the moral life, one which
is necessarily critical of other ways of construing ethics.
Here we will examine ways in which our understandings of
ethics may be corrupted in the broader American culture in
which Christians live. Christian ethics, we have argued, is
essentially concerned with making appropriate response to
what God is doing in the swirl of forces acting upon us. It is
an ethic that puts primary emphasis on the activity of God
and on human capacity for discernment, or interpretation,
in Niebuhr's terms. The stories Christians tell about Israel's
call and the life and death of Jesus give them great hope
that whatever "God is doing," it is for the purpose of human
conversion and reconciliation. Yet Christians, like everyone
else, are subject to the perennial danger of subscribing to a
view of ethics that is a response to other perceptions of the
way the world is.

The contemporary context in which American Christians are attempting to make response is one of pro-
nounced individualism. Daniel Callahan calls the morality
shaped by these forces a "minimalistic ethic" in which one's
sole obligation is to avoid harming others.[18] Besides this
minimal obligation to one another, morality is construed in
decidedly self-serving terms. We will briefly consider two

such self-serving attitudes. Both turn out to be responses not to what God is providentially doing but to what we fear is happening or will happen to us.

The first such corrupt view of ethics is fed by the desire for greater control over our lives. We want to be more "effective" people and are concerned with self-improvement—which usually translates as gaining greater control over our lives and the lives of others. But a view of morality as a quest for greater self-autonomy and less vulnerability is corrupt. In such a view freedom is understood as the capacity for becoming as independent as possible from the limitations arising from relationships with others and from historical boundedness. Because other people and our own histories keep us from accomplishing our goals we must be freed of them.

Another misunderstanding about the moral life is conspicuous at a time when nuclear annihilation is a growing real possibility. Rather than attempting to understand what God is doing as the first step toward discerning what our response ought to be, we think that we alone hold the key to the world's survival. We imagine ourselves to be the saviors of the world—and our enemies to be its destroyers. Such a view denies that God has dominion over the creation. Instead, we are in charge, and the fate of the earth is in our hands. The purpose of ethics becomes the aversion of global disaster. As with all other threats, from rampant crime to disintegration of family and community, we must find the means of saving ourselves. Ethical reflection inspired by fear is well illustrated in the writings of Jonathan Schell. In *The Fate of the Earth* Schell combines vivid descriptions of nuclear catastrophe with exhortations to forgive, trust, disarm, curb scientism, and work for the formation of world government. The message is finally that we must do these things in order to avoid self-destruction.[19] If disaster can be prevented, however, we will all be able to return to our own projects and go our individual ways. While Schell is not uninterested in having us become better people living in mutual trust, his pressing message is "reform or perish!"

While these two notions of ethics prevent us from seeing the moral task rightly, there are other corruptions more directly related to the practice of Christian morality which lead us away from rather than toward the experience of God. In their desire to honor God and God's law, Christians may be preoccupied with the law and come to view God as the distant and avenging divine judge. The deep chasm of separation is difficult to bridge: the presence of God can only be felt as law rather than as love. Efforts to abide by the law may have as their reward not God but "moralism," the attitude that through our own efforts we alone are meritorious. Losing sight of God's graciousness, even darker possibilities arise. We may grow to hate others for their unworthiness and to imagine "the support of a justifying God, an avenging and destroying spirit," since it is "easier to serve the hate-gods because one has only to be blinded by collective passion."[20] Staying on "good terms" with God may indicate an arrested spiritual development simply because God remains distant, and is mediated only through the law.

Let us consider once again Christian ethics as response to God who desires holiness. Our primary identity is that of persons-in-relation-to-others. Our moral strivings all center on the deepening capacity for friendship and for living justly. Our moral vocation is not to be better moral decision-makers but to be true friends and avid doers of justice. But we often see life as other than "with others." It is much fragmented because of our fisheye view of things. Merton reminds us of our neediness:

> As long as we are not purified by the love of God and transformed into Him in the union of pure sanctity, we will remain apart from one another, opposed to one another, and union among us will be a precarious and painful thing, full of labor and sorrow and without lasting cohesion.[21]

His words are also a reminder of the connection between spiritual growth and life with others. The experience of God's love gives us a new vision of the world and other persons. Through the power of divine love, our reason, our wills, and our freedom are redeemed. As we become more attentive, our self-preoccupation is lessened and our awareness of others and *the* Other expanded. In our attentiveness to one another we participate in each other's transformation in holiness. Together in and through God's love we recognize that the moral invitation is the call to be friends with God and to befriend one another.

The central commandments revealed in the New Testament are that we should love God with all our heart, mind, and soul and love our neighbors as ourselves. But how are we to break out of our separateness and find the source of love? The commands to love God and neighbor are a call to discern more fully the true nature of God and of ourselves. For as Thomas Merton reminds us, it is in this kind of discernment that our ability to love is grounded:

> Love is my true identity. To find love I must enter into the sanctuary where it is hidden: which is the essence of God. And to enter into his sanctity I must become holy as He is holy, perfect as He is perfect. None of this can be achieved by any effort of my own, by any strivings of my own, by any competition with other men. It means leaving all the ways that men can follow or understand. But if He sends His own love, Himself, to act and love

in me and in all that I do, then I shall be transformed, I
shall discover who I am and shall possess my true identity by losing myself in Him. And that is what is called
sanctity.[22]

Our moral vision bears fruit only when it is borne on our
desire to enter into the sanctity of God where we will know
him and in knowing him know ourselves and "all the others
who are identified with [him]."[23]

The question we must ask in all our outer striving, inner
struggling, ways of living with others, and in our deciding
and acting is finally this: Are our ways of living and those
things to which we are devoting ourselves drawing us closer
to the Holy One? In the midst of all of the ways in which we
are investing our energies comes the call to holiness. To
respond to that call is to be empowered to go deeper into
the heart of the world, becoming more fully alive and more
appreciative of life shared with others. To respond to that
call is to receive new enthusiasm (literally, to be infused by
God) for the quality of life—our own and one another's.

The objection might be raised that to link morality
to holiness is to confuse the ends of religion and morality.
The call to holiness might seem to be a religious aspiration
that functions as a reason for being moral, with "the moral"
confined to the task of making people decent rather than
saintly. Some may wonder if the attainment of holiness is
too lofty an expectation for most Christians. Is there not
some intermediate, more attainable goal of the Christian
moral life? Indeed, we might prefer a morality which seems
more within our human grasp, for fear that failure to reach
so high a goal will cause us to lose heart. We have already
noted that transformation is the birthright of all Christians
rather than the vocation of only those in the religious and
monastic life. The Scriptures tell the story of an offer made

to everyone to enter the kingdom. Only by recognizing our divine destiny is the nature of the present task to be adequately understood. It is misleading to make so sharp a distinction between the religious and the moral life. Indeed the Christian vision of God fuses what have traditionally been separated: the religious and the moral, the sacred and profane, the spiritual and the practical.

There is one objection which may be legitimately raised and which stands as a continuous warning against the possibilities of self-righteousness. Holiness and human perfection may mean very different things in terms of both their points of departure and their final destination. When "human perfection" is used to refer to what human beings strive to accomplish on their own rather than to what God is doing in them it means something fundamentally different from holiness. In fact, to speak of holiness rather than perfection may remind us that we are talking first of all about an attribute and activity of God which comes to us as gift. Indeed, H. Richard Niebuhr was reluctant to link morality and spirituality because of the dangers of self-righteousness. His Protestant heritage made him skeptical of asceticism for fear it would lead its practitioners to seek a haven safe from the world. Such detachment Niebuhr correctly considered to be both an evasion of the process of discernment of what God is doing in the tumult of worldly life and an evasion of making appropriate responses to it.

This account of the moral life anticipates that binding it so tightly to the religious quest will raise a serious question for some people. Are we saying that being holy is a precondition for being moral? Does this account of Christian morality suggest that only the spiritually committed are capable of moral response or that only those who make an explicit religious confession can possess an understanding of the moral life? These questions do point to a legitimate cause for concern that such a view of morality might exclude a great many people. What appears to be at stake is whether all human beings by virtue of their humanity share similar moral knowledge, however different in kind or intensity their religious outlooks happen to be. For without such a common morality, the argument goes, moral cooperation would not be possible. In saying that holiness is what we most need we acknowledge that without the experience of God (available in so many unexpected moments) we can do very little for ourselves or for others. With it we are known and recognize our likeness to others. And such knowledge is the foundation of an authentic morality.

Summary

We have described Christian ethics as an activity of responding to the ways in which God is acting. Our response requires interpretation; hence, we must continually discipline ourselves in the practice of discernment. The stories Christians tell about the wondrous deeds of God aid them in understanding what God is presently doing. They help to place us in the ongoing history of a provident God in whom we can trust. The Christian understanding of morality includes a particular account of moral agency in which persons are recognized as existing fundamentally in relation to God. This identity, in turn, determines how they are related to one another. Christians are called throughout their lives to holiness, which Merton refers to most simply as the imitation of the ways of God. Such imitation is described by Jesus in the Sermon on the Mount and exemplified by the quality of his own life.

Aquinas writes that human acts are motivated by the desire for happiness, the ultimate happiness being communion with God. Human activity depends upon reason's guidance of the will; however, the effect of sin has been to impair such reason. Sin is our alienation from God which produces a distorted view of the world, one in which the self now occupies center stage and cannot recognize the interests of others. Resisting the power of sin is a demanding task that begins with the desire to be attentive to the rest of reality. As we will note in the next chapter, attentiveness nurtures humility, the willingness to give up some of our control and acknowledge our dependence on God.

It is important for us to understand the task of ethics rightly, knowing what "living morally well" is about. For Christians, it is surely not about "doing well by doing good"—morality for the sake of personal success. Nor is it merely about what must be done to insure our survival. Essentially, Christian morality is the ongoing response to the summons to conversion. It is the place where the seeds of the kingdom planted in us bear fruit in our love of neighbor.

4
Power

Introduction

The term "power" describes something fundamental to human existence. We experience power most basically as an energizing and animating force upon which our existence depends. We also describe our capacity to affirm our existence by acting in terms of possessing power. Hence, our human faculties are called "powers." Power is at once something which we have and something which we enact.

The term "power" has specific theological usage in the New Testament. God is the life-giving and life-sustaining power to which Jesus testifies. The same divine power that breathes life into all human beings breathes eternal life into Jesus, who in turn offers redemption to all who submit to being empowered by God. But while Jesus promises to endow his followers with power, other "principalities and powers" at war with God entice human beings to assert that their power is simply their own. The great paradox of the power we witness in Jesus is that by choosing a form of powerlessness he was filled with the power of God. Whatever security Jesus' power provided him was grounded in the recognition that his power was not his own. He was powerful for the very reason that he acknowledged his utter dependence on God's power. And for that reason the "principalities and powers" could exercise no hold over him.

The power of God is gift: that is, we are free to accept or to refuse it. The story of the fall is the story of our attempt to seize power from God and to exercise it in such ways that it is no longer the power of God empowering us but our own feeble and doomed effort to ensure our own survival. Human freedom was used to refuse God's power; thereafter, we who wanted to be free of God were no longer free. We were possessed by the power we aspired to possess. Such power only enchained the hands that tried to wield it. Now we can only ask for the grace to discern and respond to the offer of God's power which still is ours. In Section 1 we consider the power of Jesus which in turn makes a particular form of human power possible.

1. Empowerment

The focus of the biblical accounts of creation is on the One through whose power everything has come to be. At the climactic moment of the drama Yahweh God breathed empowering spirit into human beings and they became *living* beings. Beginning with Genesis, the biblical stories depict God's power as the source of all life and all authentic human power. The biblical stories also tell of the human struggle with power. When persons use their power to aggrandize themselves, they fail miserably. But when they accept themselves as vessels of divine power, no other power can defeat them. Jesus entered into the history of Israel announcing and manifesting the power of God's rule. The Gospels testify that through him God's power was present as healing, as forgiveness, and as reconciliation between the human and the divine.

The story of Jesus fasting in the desert for forty days and resisting Satan's offer of power depicts his self-abandonment into the power of God. Jesus will not produce bread to slake his own hunger, he will not force God to produce a sign on his behalf, and he will accept no earthly rule—not even over "all the kingdoms of the world" (Mt 4). He will use his power toward no self-serving end. Here is human power perfectly faithful to its divine giver.

The Lucan account affirms that Jesus emerges from the desert "with the power of the Spirit in him" (Lk 4:14). In the Gospels, Jesus' ministry of healing and imparting new life is interpreted as the "authority and power" of God (Lk 4:36), with the miracles and the signs he performs all pointing to the creative and restorative nature of God's power.

Jesus' power is rooted in the coincidence of his will with the will of the One he calls "Abba." His power is present in his humble acknowledgment of his absolute dependence upon God. H. Richard Niebuhr observes how the humility we see in Jesus

> is not the moderation of keeping one's exact place in the scale of being, but rather that of absolute dependence on God and absolute trust in Him, with the consequent ability to remove mountains. The secret of the meekness and gentleness of Christ lies in his relation to God.[1]

Typically, the counsels we hear to be humble speak only of self-denial. But what Jesus' humility holds out to us is the way to complete self-acceptance. For Jesus hears the voice of the Father, the voice of love: "This is my Son, the beloved in whom I am well pleased" (Mk 1:11). And what he has heard not only shapes his own way of life but allows others to hear God's voice. While Jesus' death plunged his disciples into despair, his resurrection brought new confidence in the power of God now being revealed.

The power Jesus has received he conferred upon his disciples. Calling the Twelve to him, he "gave them power and authority over all devils and to cure diseases, and he sent them out to proclaim the kingdom of God and to heal" (Lk 9:1-2). The great paradox of Jesus' power, with which all who would be his disciples must struggle, is that in his weakness and death God's saving power was fully present. The "poor in spirit" whom Jesus calls "blessed" are powerful because they recognize their constant need of God. As we noted in Chapter One, St. Paul places the paradox of power at the center of Christian belief and life, exhorting fellow Christians to imitate what the world judges to be Jesus' weakness and foolishness. By sharing in his cross, Jesus' disciples will have a share in the divine power in which he is invested. The Epistle to the Ephesians includes Paul's beautiful prayer that they will be transformed by the power of God to enjoy life with God:

> Out of his infinite glory, may he give you the power through the Spirit for your hidden self to grow strong, so that Christ may live in your hearts through faith, and then, planted in love and built on love, you will with all the saints have strength to grasp the breadth and the length, the height and the depth; until, knowing the love of Christ, which is beyond all knowledge, you are filled with the utter fullness of God (Eph 3:16-19).

Jesus' disciples asked him as he was preparing to leave them, "Lord, has the time come? Are you going to restore the kingdom to Israel?" Jesus replied:

> It is not for you to know times or dates . . . but you will receive power when the Holy Spirit comes on you, and

then you will be my witnesses not only in Jerusalem but
throughout Judea and Samaria, and indeed to the ends
of the earth (Acts 1:7–8).

On Pentecost day the assembled disciples, hearing "what
sounded like a powerful wind from heaven" and seeing
"what seemed like tongues of fire," were filled with the
Spirit. On that day the promise Jesus had made came in
the form of the church. The work begun on behalf of the
kingdom by Jesus was now given to his disciples with the
assurance that the Spirit would make all things possible for
them. The existence of the church testifies to the escha-
tological nature of the kingdom: the church is the presence
of Jesus' power already in the world; to the church has been
entrusted the work of bringing the kingdom to its
fullness. The church exists to witness to the presence
of God's power in the world. Its spirituality and its
moral commitment depend upon being constantly in touch
with the power of God and being faithful imitators of
the power by which the whole creation lives and moves
and has its being.

What verifies the presence of God's power in human
community is its capacity for affirming the plenitude of life
rather than holding on tightly to life and grasping for more
by taking from others. In terms of the way we relate to
others, God's power is manifested in us as we affirm each
other's lives, by seeking their presence in order to partake
of fuller life. Bernard Loomer describes two fundamentally
different ways in which we may perceive and cultivate power.[2] The first presupposes a non-communal and non-rela-
tional view of the self. In this view the aim of the self
is to become independent of others, living by means of its
own resources and forcefulness as much as possible. Power
serves the purpose of controlling and shaping everything

around us. An alternative way of understanding power begins with the acknowledgment that selfhood emerges from mutual exchanges with others. The self grows insofar as it is able to be influenced by and make room for others. Loomer terms power that both presumes and fosters separateness "unilateral" and describes it as "the ability to produce intended or desired effects in our relationships to nature or to other people."[3] The primary purpose of such power is to influence, shape, control, or manipulate others in order to produce the greatest benefit to our own perceived interests with the least possible change in ourselves. The intent to exert power unilaterally presupposes that self-actualization depends upon dominating others and resisting the possibility of being influenced by others. Loomer writes that unilateral use of power "blocks the power of the gifts others would give us out of their freedom."[4] We keep ourselves safely distanced from others.

Loomer contrasts unilateral power with a power fostering mutuality which he calls "relational power." Such "relational power" has as its source the awareness of our incompleteness and our need for the influence of others. This power invites others to bring their truth to us, trusting that the influence of others will help bring us closer to the fullness of life. Relational power requires of us a more flexible sense of self, less certitude, and a more tentative view of reality. Relational power grows as we learn to receive others as gifts and to be open to rather than threatened by what they bring into our lives.

The "unilateral" power that Loomer describes is the sort with which we are all too familiar. It is adversarial in nature. Merton reserved some of his strongest social criticism for the unilateral shape of power so characteristic of Western society. The impulse to dominate, he wrote, has produced a spurious unity "of those thrown together without love and without understanding by the accidents of the power struggle."[5] All are drawn into the struggle, Merton continues, for "the weak must submit to the strong and join him in his adventures so that they may share in his power." Merton saw as an aspect of our contemplative growth the renunciation of "this obsession with the triumph of the individual and collective will to power."[6]

Authentic "power," Loomer argues, is always relational. Whatever genuine power people possess arises from mutual exchange with others. In all of our relationships, marriage and parenting, work and play, social advocacy and international relations, we are involved in patterns which tend either in the direction of the mutuality or toward patterns of domination and submission that crush the human spirit.

The relational exercise of power might seem to be an impossible ideal once one moves beyond close personal relationships into broader social contexts. Indeed, unilateral power so dominates local and national politics and relations among nations that nothing else seems possible. We may desire for our personal relationships to be ones in which relational power operates and yet believe that we must relate "differently" in other contexts. But we cannot sustain two different styles of power. At any one time, one form of power will be growing more characteristic of our relationships with all others, whether near or far. Our great challenge is to be the same persons in the private and the public domains of our lives. We look to the church to school us in the authentic use of power.

2. Stories About Power

What often keeps us from the relational exercise of power are the stories we tell about ourselves that make us appear "different" from (that is, "better" than) other people. Because God had made a covenant with Israel, calling it to give its exclusive fidelity and promising it great blessings in return, the Israelites were tempted to feel superior to other nations. But their own national story would not let them do so for long insofar as it was a story of their repeated infidelity. Alone among ancient epics, the history of Israel does not celebrate the personal valor or goodness of the Israelites. Indeed, the biblical writers sharply contrasted the faint-heartedness and failure of the people with the fidelity and forgiveness of Yahweh, who alone is worthy of admiration and worship. By telling the story of Yahweh's covenant-making with them Israel could not be allowed to forget who was to be revered—and who continually needed to repent for being unfaithful to the covenant! No doubt all subsequent generations who acknowledged these stories as their own would have liked to revise them in the direction of a more complimentary self-identity. The amended version would predictably have attributed to the people themselves most of the credit for their success, with God playing only a peripheral role. Any accounts of their failures would not make them look bad but only at times erring (since the whole object is to leave their goodness unquestioned).

In this section we will examine three stories we as Americans tell about ourselves that condition us to practice a unilateral form of power. To each of these stories we will juxtapose one of Israel's stories that served to remind it of the condition of its existence. Such stories have the power to remind us of our condition. The American stories are not uniquely pernicious ones. For like other peoples, we are tempted when we tell our stories to make ourselves out to be the central heroes. What national epic except for Israel's does not aggrandize the virtues and minimize the vices of the people and the ancestors they celebrate?

Self-Made in America

A strong motif in the American story is that by our own industriousness and hard work we can guarantee our own success. Indeed our ancestors worked hard and reaped a bountiful harvest from the earth. From them we inherited an abiding faith in progress and success. Wave on wave of immigrants came, poor boys like Horatio Alger who would pull themselves up from their poverty by their own bootstraps to heights of power and wealth. The possibilities were limitless, prosperity awaiting those who were willing to do an honest day's work.

Even in the midst of a faltering economy that now has denied prosperity and brought crisis for millions of Americans, even as we are being called to recognize and respect the limits of growth, we still believe that the prize still goes to the industrious and that only the lazy fail. We still hold as an article of faith that it is our particular ingenuity that makes the earth bloom and the production lines move. Believing ourselves to be "self-made," we fail to acknowledge the Giver of the gifts—not to mention the labors of others that may have been unjustly gotten.

Alexis de Tocqueville reported a dark side of the prosperity he observed in his travels in America in the 1830s. He wrote of encountering a restlessness, a competitiveness, and a certain sadness among Americans. Such a spirit, he suggested, stemmed from the apparent fact that they "never stop thinking of the good things they have not got."[7] "They clutch everything," he wrote, "but hold nothing fast."[8] Americans now as then are a very future-oriented people, who for all their outward self-confidence and pride in what they have accomplished are quite unsure about the present worth of themselves and their lives. Ironically, commitment to the idea of progress may not only reflect our past success but also reflect present dissatisfaction over who we are and what we have done, causing us to look anxiously to the future in search of selves we can better understand and accept. For now, working hard—even at playing—serves to distract us from what makes us unhappy about ourselves.

If we are unable to think of anything else than "the good things we have not got," we will be both ungrateful for the gifts we have been given and not inclined to share them with others. Indeed, if it were true that our success depended solely on our own ingenuity and industriousness, we would have good reason to fear failure and focus all of our powers in all-out competitive war against all others who might succeed at the cost of our failure. We might say that our competitiveness was only part of the sport of it, part of the fun of playing the game. Yet we would sacrifice everything to win, believing this to be a game of life or death.

As the Israelites were being led to the promised land they too were tempted to believe more in their own deservedness than in the gracious power of God. What they have been freely given they are wont to deny to the needy among them—and that tendency was only to increase once they became a prosperous kingdom. Despite all they have been given they too grumbled for more. Indeed, God's warning to Israel has a contemporary relevance about it:

> Beware lest you say in your heart, "My power and the might of my hand have gotten me this wealth." You shall remember the Lord your God, for it is he who gives you power to get wealth; that he may confirm his covenant which he swore to your fathers, as at this day (Dt 8:17–18).

The Autonomous Self

A century and half ago Tocqueville wrote of a certain American characteristic and even coined a word with which to designate it. "Individualism" as he described it is

> a calm and measured feeling which disposes each
> citizen to isolate himself from the mass of his fellows
> and withdraw into the circle of family and friends; with
> this little society formed to his taste, he gladly leaves the
> greater society to look after itself.[9]

In their landmark study of the search by Americans for self
and community Robert Bellah and his team of researchers
describe the advanced stages of such individualism. *Habits
of the Heart* laments how the individualism which has
shaped American life has made it difficult for us to think
about ourselves as anything but "arbitrary centers of voli-
tion" or to actualize the fullness of our being.[10]

In Michael Sandel's phrase, individuals striving to be
"unencumbered selves" feel little connection with or responsibility for others.[11] The portrait of society they form is
of individuals isolated from each other and keeping their
values to themselves in the belief that it is not possible to
expect others to share what are inherently private visions of
life. As Tocqueville characterizes them,

> Such folk owe no man anything and hardly expect any-
> thing from anybody. They form the habit of thinking of
> themselves in isolation and imagine that their whole
> destiny is in their hands. . . . Each man is forever thrown
> back on himself alone, and there is danger that he may
> be shut up in the solitude of his own heart.[12]

The biblical creation account offers a very different
understanding of the person and of community. God has
created finite persons of infinite worth. They have been en-
dowed with freedom in order that they might respond to
the divine summons to share in the divine life. Each is wonderfully made; all are made for one another's company.
The worst privation human beings can experience is that of

being barred from the common life, unable to participate in the life of the community. The worst kind of self-deprivation is to imagine that others have nothing to do with completing what is lacking in ourselves. The Genesis creation story affirms that human beings are created to be with one another rather than to be alone. They are on a journey together—not simply stranded together as Beckett portrays Vladimir and Estragon.

True community respects the uniqueness of each person as a gift to be received and respected. Unlike a totality which aims at leveling all distinctions among persons, a community welcomes and draws life from the diversity of its members. Rather than seeking conformity, a community fosters the self-realization of each of the persons who comprise it. Each is encouraged to take responsibility for the freedom each has been given, not with the aim of becoming self-reliant, but for the purpose of making the journey to themselves to discover precisely the persons God intends them to be. Christianity professes that only by recognizing their own identity and discovering the manner in which God is uniquely revealed to them at their own center can persons work out their salvation. Those who are on the journey toward self-discovery are able to affirm and support the journey of other selves whom God has made and called to self-realization.

Of Innocence

Perhaps the most harmful story a people can tell about themselves is that they are blissfully innocent. Nineteenth century America felt itself to be the New Eden, freed from the sins of its European past. Mary Collins, a contemporary religious educator, speaks of the myth of innocence that forms our cultural bedrock, providing an "earthly paradise motif for the American psyche" in which "the opportunity to begin life again in a new land had meant leaving every-thing behind, including the sin of the old world, including original sin."[13] She warns that in such a myth "there is no place in the cultural imagination . . . that Americans as Americans are implicated in the sin of the world."[14] Such an attitude bred the belief in our nation's manifest destiny to carry our way of life abroad. It continues to fuel the convic-tion that we are the righteous ones called by God to do his work.

Two decades ago the destruction wrought by the Viet-nam War made Americans painfully aware of our lack of innocence. We would have preferred to believe that the evil in the world was largely perpetrated by the communists, or the agitators, or the malcontents. We tried to refute the charge of our own destructiveness, arguing that only a mi-nority of pathological personalities in our society exhibit such violence; for the rest, violence is required for the protection of decency and humanity. We were resolved to silence all those who accused us of evil-doing and did not lack the firepower to do so. Indeed, we had become very dangerous to others and to ourselves. Paradise was under siege and Collins describes our reaction:

> 'It's not my fault,' we protest. 'Leave me alone.' We kick, punch, stomp and shout. Get rid of one, somebody else shows up, always dogging us. . . . A way of life which accuses and threatens us has no right to exist; it invites annihilation. The spasms of violent reaction which have seized us are symptoms of a soul sickness, as virulent as the disorder we resist. Here is mortal sin to fit the name! It can destroy us and the whole planet with us unless we can get our seizures under control. But how?[15]

It was in Vietnam and back home that we were forced to draw near to suffering and pain and guilt that belies our innocence. A decade after the U.S. brought its troops home voices and images still haunted us and challenged our "innocence." We preferred to forget about the war, but grieving families, angry and alienated veterans, and the presence of Amerasian children did not let us.

Getting beyond the illusions of innocence requires acknowledging guilt and seeking forgiveness and reconciliation. Collins describes the controversial Vietnam War Memorial in Washington, D.C. as evoking in those who experience it a painful truth about the war and about themselves. The memorial consists of two long and low walls of black marble carved into the sides of a rise in the earth and facing each other. On the walls are etched the names of the fifty-nine thousand American war dead. Unlike other war memorials, this one does not celebrate heroism but conveys a sense of human suffering and loss. Collins describes her reaction to it:

> Whoever moves within close range of its two long wings . . . hears a quiet insistent question: what about this suffering? A young Asian American woman, Maya Lin, dared us, through her memorial design, to look at suffering, to come close enough to see its human scale, and to see our own faces dimly reflected in the highly polished marble wall. The place is dangerous. In its ambience, we could be moved to forgive one another.[16]

Seeing our reflections in the blackness of that wall we are bidden to come to terms with the dark unconscious forces acting upon us. Facing the war memorial walls, Collins was moved to grieve for what our illusions of power had wrought. "Where," she asked, "are there enough polished marble *memorials to powerlessness* that we could all come closer, see the pain and defeat, recognize our own faces dimly, and risk asking forgiveness?"[17] Indeed, all of the stories of Israel and of Jesus remind us that despite our sinfulness God loves us. Because of the very nature of our God we can dare to seek forgiveness and to hope that beyond our failure lies the possibility of new life.

Our great challenge as Christians is to recognize our own stories in the stories of Israel and to resist making our own national stories into our "bible." For the stories of God's covenant-making with Israel would not support illusions of industriousness, independence, and innocence. Stories of a sinless past requiring no repentance and of moving ahead by our own steam cannot stand up to the ancient story of Israel. The power of the God whom that story proclaims is so provident that we need not work so hard to secure our future. And the God of that story is so forgiving that we can dare to ask for forgiveness. Our God—and not our own story—is unique. We must resist or revise the stories of our alleged innocence, industriousness, and autonomy in order that we can recognize "how like we are to those about whom the tale [of Israel] is told [and] how like we are to all who with us listen to the tale."[18]

3. The Temptation of Power

The age-old question is whether human beings can afford to risk living a "relational" form of power by which we trust the influence of others to take us to fuller life. Is not our unilateral power warranted to put limits on the excessive displays of unilateral power that utterly disregard the dignity and worth of other selves? Are we not warranted, in exceptional instances, to seek to control the aggressive onslaughts of others? Must we not use or threaten to use violence against those who are perpetrating injustice?

In the matter of power, we are from the start involved in a contradiction. However much we may aspire to learn relational power, we are members of political communities that maintain their authority by the threat to use coercive power against any who would not comply with its laws. Even though such communities rely largely upon voluntary cooperation, they also depend as a last resort on the employment of violence. The threat of violence is viewed as a necessity for the maintenance of political authority, even though it is a two-edged sword that when used carelessly undermines political authority and destroys political community.

Christians live in a state of constant tension, participants in political communities maintained by coercive power and yet members of another community called to grow in the love of God by welcoming the stranger and the stranger's truth into their lives. Christians are called to conform their lives to a power that is creative rather than destructive, which reknits the human community rather than deepening the enmity that now divides it. Amidst a world that largely subscribes to power as coercion, they must struggle to enact the power of love in their personal relationships and in their politics. Whether they hold pacifist convictions or the view that inflicting harm on others may under exceptional circumstances be justified as the choice of the lesser evil in the pursuit of justice, they must struggle to witness to the power of the kingdom.[19]

Discussions of power among Christians often revolve around the issue of whether a non-violent pacifist strategy is an appropriate response when coercive power is being unjustly imposed by others. Can relational power really redeem such a situation? Will the evil only be multiplied by Christians submitting themselves to it? In the late 1930s, at a time of great international anxiety over Japan's aggression in the Far East, H. Richard Niebuhr gave concrete application to his vision of the moral life as "fitting response" to the divine activity revealed in human history. Niebuhr's assessment of what the fitting response of American Christians might be prompted an exchange of views between him and his brother, Reinhold. It remains a remarkable exchange, revealing two very different visions of how much of God's power can penetrate human history and of how Christians must employ power in anticipation of the coming of the fullness of God's reign.

In the midst of deepening international tensions H. Richard counseled a particular sort of "inactivity" based on the faith that something *is* being done "which is divine both in its threat and its promise."[20] The "meaningful inactivity" he commended was not founded on a pessimistic view that there was nothing worth doing. Nor was it based on a belief that we could assume the role of righteous spectators looking on while evil men did their bullying. Instead, Niebuhr urged his fellow American Christians to respond first by recognizing how much their own behavior resembled that of Japan and by repenting of their own aggression and racism at home and abroad.[21] Niebuhr saw the times as an opportunity for Christians to "build cells of those in each nation," who reject nationalistic fervor and "unite in a higher loyalty which transcends national and class lines of division and prepares for the future."[22] The present situation, he concluded, "is likely to result in some surprising discoveries as to the amount of renunciation of self-interest necessary on the part of this country and of individual Christians before anything effective can be done in the east."[23]

Reinhold Niebuhr agreed with his brother that the seeds of the present Japanese aggression had been sown by Western imperialism. He also conceded that Christians ought to at all times be striving for self-renunciation and humility. But Reinhold rejected the view of love underlying his brother's view of what ought to be done. He argued that an ethic based on love which does not have room for the necessity of coercion is unworkable in human history, given our sinful human nature. By faith, he said, we may experience non-coercive power "in anticipatory terms," but such power is not the basis for a constructive ethic. Violence remains the necessary means by which self-interested groups resist the excessive selfishness of other groups. He concluded: "Love may qualify the social struggle of history but it will never abolish it, and those who attempt to bring society under the dominion of perfect love will die on the cross."[24]

In his rejoinder H. Richard Niebuhr rejected his brother's tragic view of history and reaffirmed the possibility for human fulfillment that "can only be designated as 'love.'"[25] He again recommended as preparatory for the kingdom of God an exercise of human power that resists self-interest and self-assertion. Our "inactivity," he insisted, is to be a time of grace in which repentance and forgiveness could occur. H. Richard did not underestimate the power of sin. But he also saw in the cross the actualizing in history of the power of divine grace. Hence he testified to the power of divine love as more than "an ambulance driver in the wars of interested and clashing parties."[26]

Reinhold Niebuhr was deeply aware of the "tragic" nature of history due to both human sinfulness and the violence necessary to resist the evil of some so that others might be spared from still greater suffering. Insofar as we trust that grace is at work in the world transforming it to its original unity and harmony, then "preventive" violence is no longer perceived as either our obligation or our sole tragic option. Such a faith empowers us to discover greater life by the commitment to live peaceably, with compassion, receptivity, and humility, waiting patiently in joyful hope for the coming of the kingdom.

Striving to exercise this kind of power will of course not be easy. As pacifists or as just war adherents we will continue to be faced with much moral ambiguity and uncertainty as to what our fitting response should be. But by the Spirit all power has been given us which frees us from the heavy burden of "making history come out right." Rather, in the struggle to discern and to imitate God's power we believe that we will be transformed by it.

4. The Fire of Love

The chief way in which the Christian tradition speaks of its experience of the creating, redeeming, and transforming power of God is by proclaiming the power of divine love. The First Letter of John eloquently describes the work of divine love:

> We ourselves have known and put our faith in God's love toward ourselves. God is love and anyone who lives in love lives in God, and God lives in him. Love will come to its perfection in us when we can face the day of judgment without fear; because even in this world we have become as he is. In love there can be no fear, but fear is driven out by perfect love. . . . We are to love because he loved us first (1 Jn 4:16–19).

John makes the "order" of love clear: by first loving us God has enabled us to love. Merton stressed the importance of remembering this order of things, writing: "The root of Christian love is not the will to love, but *the faith that one is loved*. The faith that one is loved *by God*."[27]

Refusing to believe that we are truly lovable is the great impediment to loving others.

"Love" is so dominant a notion in Christian theology that in the New Testament four Greek words, *eros, philia, agape* and *caris*, are used to describe the manifestations of divine love. In the Hebrew Bible the word *chesed*, often translated as "loving kindness," connotes God's solicitousness, self-giving, fidelity, and mercy toward Israel. Vilma Seelaus describes the biblical faith of the Jews in a loving and compassionate God, saying:

> As the People of Israel told and retold their stories . . . a very profound Biblical anthropology as well as theology emerged. They not only discovered God present in their history, they also discovered themselves—they were a people peculiarly His own. . . . The openness to the transcendent felt by primitive peoples throughout the ages has a specific meaning for us. We are called to dwell with the Holy One, our creator who marvelously invites us to a relationship of intimacy.[28]

This faith in the power of a loving and compassionate God is the essence of Christianity as well.

Our love of other people and things always verges on the desire to possess them or at least to judge them to be significant only insofar as they are useful to us. How are we to resist the centripetal force of our lives by which we pull everything and everyone toward ourselves? Merton spoke of the imperfection of our love that arises from the

> disorder of our desire that looks for . . . a greater fulfillment than any created thing is capable of giving. Instead of worshipping God through His creation we are always trying to worship ourselves by means of creatures.[30]

Only God can cure our insatiable hungers. Merton commends as our only true joy

> enter[ing] by love into union with the Life Who dwells and sings within the essence of every creature and in the core of our own souls. In His love we possess all things and enjoy fruition of them, finding Him in them all.[31]

We are faced with two options: either to strive to save ourselves—and by violence if necessary—or to accept that we rest secure in God's immense love for us. Repentance begins with the overwhelming loss of confidence in the first option. Such "breakdowns" often border on despair but turn out to be moments of "breakthroughs" in which the good news of God's forgiveness is finally heard and accepted. A powerful impetus for repentance is the experience of vulnerability and failure. In the midst of repentance comes the experience of being forgiven and recognizing our likeness to others whereby we can forgive each other. Repentance opens the way to authentic self-discovery.

Repentance is a painful process. It is no wonder that metaphors of fire are often used to speak of the attainment of holiness: through repentance the fire of God's love cleanses us of our false self-images. Repentance is the demanding discipline of inviting a new power in to displace the power that once reigned. Repentance brings us to the point of receptive silence. We need not speak on our own behalf but only to listen. Into the void of our guilt and powerlessness comes the message of forgiveness and the release of another power in our lives to heal us and bring us together.

Through faith in love and love's Source we are enabled to draw near to God and to others. Love's object is no longer absent. The stranger becomes recognizable as a neighbor. Recognition of being loved allows the self to no longer force its claims upon the world. In its growing appreciation of how good all creation is for being loved by God, the self naturally becomes self-forgetful. The connection between the virtue of love and our spiritual growth is inseparable. Belief in God's love for us and our consequent ability to love others as we ourselves are loved is the way of human perfection. Growth in the virtue of love brings increasing harmony between God, self, and neighbor. Again, Merton suggests the power of God's gift of love:

> The more I become identified with God, the more I will be identified with the others who are identified with Him. His love will live in all of us. And we shall love one another and God with the same love with which He loves us and Himself.[32]

Reinhold Niebuhr, we recall, claimed that love could not be the basis of a constructive social ethic. But Christians have grounds for believing that the potency of a nonviolent love will prevail to reconcile brothers and sisters, husbands and wives, blacks and whites, communists and capitalists. As the incarnation of God's love, Jesus is the promise and the fulfillment of reconciliation. All that the Christian tradition affirms about love originates and returns to God, since it is God's love that gives us and everything else existence. All of our movements of love arise in the divine movement of love. For God first loved us into existence. We are the beloved. Our experiences of forgiveness and empowerment for shared life finally have the same character as the experience of love received: they are gifts. Our gratitude is measured by our commitment to imitate the love of God through our effort to cultivate the kind of power that builds up a community to impart the love of God to others.

The church's task is to make such power incarnate in the world and credible to it. This it does by the love its members show for one another and by their commitment to make their love universal. In H. Richard Niebuhr's words, the churches are the "cells" of people preparing for the fullness of the kingdom by their repentance and their resolve to bring reconciliation and unity to a world now divided. The work goes on as one by one people find the divisions in and among themselves being healed. Sometimes the process is readily discernible: witness, for example, the struggle of blacks in America under the leadership of Martin Luther King, Jr., to heal the nation of three centuries of racism. Here it was the practice of the power of non-violent love by black church communities—and then timidly by white churches—that healed division and made brotherhood a reality.

Summary

This chapter has considered human power in relation to its divine source and has explored how it may be faithful to the Empowerer. Images of ourselves and our power form the foundation of our moral and spiritual lives. We have suggested that power is relational and that through mutuality our lives are enlarged. To trust ultimately in the power of God, a power revealed paradoxically as weakness, leads to being empowered by God. Humility is the mark of such empowerment. Conversely, to trust only in our own power often leads to violence because it suggests that we are alone and have nothing but ourselves to rely upon.

The power necessary to repent, to seek forgiveness, to love and to live non-violently is not easily acquired. Even to describe power in this way most of the time runs counter to our sense of the world. How can we grow in this kind of power? Since it is not power that we can lay claim to as "ours," all we can do is to make ourselves available to receive it by joining in the work of the community which Jesus empowered with his Spirit. The most apt language for speaking of divine power is the language of love. For by the power of divine love our lives and our loves are transformed. Rosemary Haughton speaks of transformation as the "release of power" in which we are " 'taken over' by the power of the Spirit."[33] In certain prophetic personalities, she writes, this "taking over" is sudden and complete; for the rest of us it is gradual and only partially felt.

In the next chapter we will consider that "gradual and only partial" process by which Christians come into the possession of certain strengths necessary for living well. In more traditional language, the process of acquiring such strengths is the learning of the virtues.

5
The Habits of
the Christian Life

Introduction

In Chapter Three the Christian moral life was described in terms of the responsiveness to God as the source of self-knowledge and of life shared with others. Our first moral activity ought to be to discern what God is doing in our midst. Our holiness is to be found in seeking to respond fittingly to what God is doing. In the previous chapter we noted that recognizing the presence of God frees us from the seeming necessity of providing for our own security. We are enabled to believe in the power of God's love for us and can overcome the hostilities that prevent us from truly loving one another.

In this chapter we examine at greater length how the power of God can work in human life through human responses of a particular kind and character. "Morality" is often perceived as focusing on the moral decisions we are called upon to make periodically. But in fact the decisions we make (both the momentous and the minor choices) depend upon the sorts of people we have become. *Who* we are determines to a significant extent *how* we will decide in a particular instance. As we have repeatedly pointed out, discovering who we are is a spiritual journey from self-deception to self-knowledge that only knowledge of God can reveal. Responding to God forms us into a particular sort of people who will exhibit certain strengths or powers of character by the way they respond.

The traditional means of examining moral character is by considering the virtues. In the sections below we will inquire about which virtues make the lives of Jesus' disciples into a "fitting response" to what God is doing. Before focusing on specific virtues we will briefly consider the "ethics of virtue" which has long been part of Christian moral thought and received its fullest elaboration by Thomas Aquinas. We will also anticipate some of the potential problems of concentrating on the virtues before attending to the virtues of compassion, justice and mercy, hope, patience, courage, and prudence.

It is appropriate that we continue the discussion of power by taking up the virtues since "virtue" means literally the power or strength of character by which we are enabled to move toward greater wholeness of life. Examining what Aquinas thought about the virtues makes it at once clear why the subject is an important link between Christian spiritual and moral life. Aquinas speaks of *caritas* as the divine love which God gives to human beings in order that their friendship with God may be possible. He says that *caritas* directs "the acts of all other virtues to the last end . . . giv[ing] the form to all other acts of virtue."[1] That is, all of the virtues have as their goal preparing human beings for divine friendship. As the acorn contains the imprint of the oak tree into which it will grow, the virtues are all ordained to making us into friends of God. Aquinas claims that we are not naturally fitted for such friendship but that God gives us the capacity by means of grace. The virtues, then, are intended to bring us to God and also give us the capacity for community with each other. In what we will say about the virtues which Christian tradition commends we will try to stress how they work toward divine and human friendship.

It is important to keep firmly in mind the role Aquinas gave to *caritas*, lest we forget that all of our virtues come from God and serve the end of bringing us to God. The danger of an ethic of virtue is that we will think of the acquisition of virtue as a self-sculpting process in which we create and perfect ourselves. The holiness to which Christians are called is a divine gift. It is not earned—least of all when we are tempted to think we are earning it. In fact, the very character traits we will examine have the effect of loosing the chains of self-preoccupation, enlarging our capacity for fuller life with others and with God.

Though our powers depend continually on supernatural grace, we need to consider the question of whether virtues can be taught and, if so, how. Paradoxically, we learn virtues by the habitual performance of virtuous acts. Slowly, we become persons possessing certain virtues who in turn will act in a consistent manner. Primarily we are attracted to perform virtuous acts by the example of others in whom God's grace is at work. Other people and communities past and present sufficiently embody the virtues and encourage us to develop the same personal strengths. Some of them we revere as saints and heroes.

In the following discussion of the virtues of the Christian community we will seek examples of persons and communities whose lives were conspicuously graced with the presence of the virtues. Two problems arise in using examples to illustrate virtues. First, singling out one or another virtue in a particular life is artificial insofar as it is not an adequate spiritual or moral biography displaying the full depth of one's powers. Second, praising the virtues of particular persons might give the mistaken impression that they reached a point of no longer feeling the effects of sin. They would, no doubt, be the first to deny such perfection and emphasize their lifelong struggle to know and do the will of God.

While imitation is important in the learning of virtue, it is not a simple matter. The treatment of the virtues below will not attempt to answer such questions as, for example, "What do we need to do to be more compassionate or hopeful people?" Rather, the description of the virtues intends to respond to the more basic question: Why and in what sense are these particular virtues considered to be desirable traits in the tradition with which we identify ourselves? That is, how is it that these are the virtues of faithful discipleship? Aquinas' account of the virtues began with prudence, justice, temperance, and courage, the virtues classically known as the "cardinal virtues." He then proceeded to the virtues of faith, hope, and love, referred to by Christians as the "theological virtues." We will consider first the virtue of love, with which we concluded our discussion of power.

1. Love: Participation in Jesus' Compassion

Aquinas taught that the ultimate human happiness can be arrived at only by the power of God available through Christ, in whom we are made "partakers of the divine nature" (2 Pet 1:4).[2] By the divine infusion of faith, hope, and charity the human reason and will are transformed. In the previous chapter we noted that faith in God's love makes us capable of loving others. Here we will consider charity especially as it is revealed in the form of Jesus' living and dying for our salvation.

The three precepts of the natural law which Aquinas discusses in the *Summa* are all related to key aspects of what human beings value dearly and direct their wills toward preserving, namely, their own lives.[3] Aquinas notes that we desire to preserve our lives, to bear children to whom we can pass on all that life means to us, and to live in community with others. Yet in the way in which Jesus directed his will he subordinated these desires to the will of his Father. It was out of his human will that Jesus responded in the garden of Gethsemane on the eve of his passion: "Father . . . not what I will, but what you will" (Mk 14:36).

Caritas is fully present in Jesus, who expresses the fullness of divine love in dying in order to save us. The stories of his acts of compassion culminate in his act of self-sacrifice on the cross. In him we witness the divine love as a costly act of self-spending. The New Testament writers used the word *agape* to describe Jesus' sacrificial love. In his own teachings about love Jesus commands his listeners: "Love your enemies, pray for those who persecute you" (Mt 5:44). In answer to a pious Jew's question about how he might possess eternal life Jesus taught: "You must love the Lord your God with all your heart, with all your soul, with all your strength, and with all your mind, and your neighbor as yourself. Do this and life is yours" (Lk 10:27–28). When the questioner persisted by asking "And who is my neighbor?" Jesus described the apathy of the priest and Levite toward the one in need and the compassion of the Samaritan. Jesus concluded the parable with *the* significant question: "Which of these three, do you think, proved neighbor to the man who fell among robbers?" It is no longer a question of *whom* we shall regard as neighbor but rather what is required of us *as neighbor*. The parable makes clear that we are to help anyone in need, heedless of whether or not they are "one of our own kind." Jesus' teaching about compassion through the story of the good Samaritan aiding a needy Jew challenges us to exclude no group or class from our self-spending love.

Human beings exercise agapeistic love or compassion when they choose to be present to those who suffer, to comfort them and alleviate their pain. Compassion literally means suffering with others. Being compassionate requires that we draw near to their suffering rather than remain at a distance. We are not inclined to share other people's suffering. In fact we flee from suffering whenever we can, having many strategies for avoiding pain. We may resign ourselves in the belief that we are quite powerless to help ease the pain that others experience. We may even defensively blame them or claim it isn't our doing. We may try to help them but withdraw if they appear ungrateful by rebuffing our attempts to comfort them.

Our courage to shoulder the suffering of others is rooted in our belief that the incarnation effected human healing by sharing in human brokenness. Merton calls our compassionate presence a healing process in which the "body of broken bones" is reknit. But he warns:

> As long as we are on earth, the love that unites us will bring us suffering by our very contact with one another. ... Even saints cannot live with saints on this earth without some anguish, without some pain of the differences that come between them.[4]

The suffering which is an inevitable part of compassion is by no means sought for its own sake. Willingness to suffer is not the same as willingly accepting humiliation. For one who is chronically humiliated soon comes to doubt his or her own worthiness and may even acquiesce in his or her own degradation. The self-loathing that follows incapacitates one from affirming the goodness of the creation.

Compassion: Dorothy Day and the
Catholic Worker Movement

Learning to be sympathetic toward others is the first step on the road to compassion. Merton wrote, "If I do not spontaneously feel . . . sympathy for others, then it is God's will that I do what I can to learn how."[5] He instructed those who desire the divine gift of contemplation that until they have learned compassion they will wait in vain for the experience of God. How can we become compassionate? The answer seems to be found in giving ourselves over to one or other of a hundred situations in which human beings are suffering around us. A most powerful impetus to learning compassion is often the uninvited suffering that visits our lives and makes us a friend to all who suffer.

The foundation and forms of Dorothy Day's compassion are worth exploring especially because she has inspired many U.S. Catholics to experience more deeply the compassion of Christ. With Peter Maurin, Dorothy Day founded the Catholic Worker Movement which for more than fifty years has been dedicated to extending compassion to thousands of homeless, hungry, and hopeless people in America and reminding Catholics of the social dimension of their faith. The Catholic Worker Movement remains a friend to the poor.

In her autobiography, *The Long Loneliness*, Day recalled how she first came to know the poor in her youthful exposure in the early 1900s to Chicago's drab factories and tenements and to poverty-stricken workers and their families.[6] She was repelled by capitalism's cruelty and saw in the Russian revolution hope for the liberation of the working class. There the activism that would characterize the rest of her life was being awakened. On later reflection she wrote that her youthful feeling toward the poor and her early socialist commitment on their behalf was not yet genuine compassion:

> And what was this love of our fellows? Certainly we
> loved them in the mass; we were moved by the accounts of their suffering, and by what we saw of their
> suffering, and our hearts burned with the desire for justice and we revolted at the idea of a doled-out charity.
> The word charity had become something to gag over,
> something to shudder at. The true meaning of the word
> we did not know.[7]

Day's capacity for active and enduring compassion was to come by way of her own personal experience of suffering stemming from two prison experiences. The first occurred in 1917 when she was arrested during a suffragist demonstration at the White House and with several other women received a thirty-day prison sentence. In prison they were subjected to both physical and mental abuse by prison authorities and protested by means of a week-long hunger strike. In addition to her own suffering and humiliation, what she saw in prison had a powerful effect on her. She wrote:

> I would never be free again, never free when I knew
> that behind bars all over the world there were women
> and men, young girls and boys, suffering . . . for crimes
> of which all of us were guilty. . . . I was the mother
> whose child had been raped and slain. I was the mother
> who had borne the monster who had done it. I was
> even that monster, feeling in my own breast every
> abomination.[8]

Day suffered an even more bitter prison experience in 1922. During a police raid on a socialist party headquarters in Chicago she was falsely accused of prostitution and briefly jailed, this time not with socially prominent suffragists but with prostitutes, petty criminals, and the emotionally disturbed. She was deeply humiliated by the accusation. Thirty years later it was still painful to recall the experience in her autobiography. She was devastated by the accusation and in that "solitary taste of injustice" she recalled experiencing "as never before, the life of the poorest of the poor, the guilty, the dispossessed."[9] Her sympathy for the poor ignited into flames of compassion by what she felt within those jail walls for all who suffered within the slum walls.

It would be a distortion of Dorothy Day's life to fail to mention the experience of profound joy which was central to her own conversion. In 1927 she gave birth to a daughter, Tamara. About that experience she wrote: "No human creature could receive or contain so vast a flood of love and joy as I felt after the birth of my child. With this came the need to worship."[10] It was the experience of such love that brought her to the Catholic Church and made her capable of enduring love for the poor. Her decision to have Tamara baptized and to become a Catholic herself soon spelled the end of her common-law marriage to a man supremely suspicious of religion.

In 1932 she met Peter Maurin, a French Catholic immigrant with the social vision she hungered for but which she had not yet found in Catholicism. Inspired by Maurin's spirit and ideas (and with almost no other resources than Maurin's encouragement) Day undertook to publish a newspaper, *The Catholic Worker*, espousing a life of voluntary poverty as the solution to human want. It was the height of the Depression and Maurin was soon bringing homeless people to the *Worker* office to spend the night, literally turning it overnight into a house of hospitality.

Many others were attracted to their work and came to help with the paper and dish out the soup, some permanently, others for a time, others on vacation from work, college, and seminary. In the 1940s other Catholic Worker Houses, as they were called, were established. In addition to supporting the cause of workers and the poor, *The Catholic Worker* began what has become an unceasing protest against militarism, the cold war, and the nuclear arms race. Maurin died in 1949 and Day carried on the work until her death in 1980. She and her co-workers provided the poor, the ill and the outcast of New York with bread, soup, a bed, and compassion. She lived for nearly fifty years in the Catholic Worker House in the Bowery, frequently visiting other Worker Houses and a Worker farm established on Long Island.

Dorothy Day believed that it was not enough to offer alms or sympathy to the needy from a distance, saying, "One must live with them, share with them their suffering too. Give up one's privacy, and mental and spiritual comforts as well as physical."[11] She chose to share their suffering as the means of alleviating it. The suffering she had tasted had united her to their suffering. Her compassion stemmed from the belief that by sharing their suffering and offering them solace she would know the love of God and bring it to greater fruition in God's good creation. Her earlier personal experience of the poor's suffering, her experience of God's love, and Maurin's conviction that the genius and goodness of the people only needed to be tapped made her a friend of the the poor. Presumably many others were attracted to the movement because of similar experiences. By the 1960s Catholic Workers were operating more than forty houses of hospitality in response to the urban needy across the country.

Day resisted praise for her work of compassion and

peacemaking, saying only that she did what the Gospel mandated all of us to do. Yet, she did it with such conviction and constancy that her life became an example of compassion not only to those who were drawn to the Catholic Worker Movement but to the whole Church to which she had converted as a young woman. Her ability to love was attended by a good deal of humility. She did not criticize those who did not choose her way as one who is overly certain that there is no other way. Her writing includes passages in which she questioned the effectiveness of some of her means of working for justice. Yet her love and respect was evident for those in the wider Church who found her message too radical to endorse (her pacifism, for example), and not a few Catholic bishops sought her counsel. In the familiar hymn found in Paul's First Letter to the Corinthians, love is described as the foundation of the virtues:

> Love is always patient and kind; it is never rude or selfish; it does not take offense, and is not resentful. Love takes no pleasure in other people's sin but delights in the truth; it is always ready to excuse, to trust, to hope, and to endure whatever comes (1 Cor 13:4–7).

2. Justice

While love calls us to recognize the worthiness of all, justice obliges us to recognize the particularity of others, and especially to acknowledge their specific needs. "Justice properly speaking," declares Aquinas, "demands a distinction of parties."[12] Since justice requires honoring the legitimate claims and needs of others, it is necessary that we recognize others as selves separate from us. Josef Pieper goes so far as to say that in a justice mode of relating we confront each other "almost as strangers."[13] But it is an inadequate conception of justice which would have us "keeping our distance" from one another so that exploitation does not find an opportunity. For the presence of justice allows us to become an authentic community by urging us to honor in its members what is uniquely their own and worthy of respect.

An adequate conception of justice requires us to consider the nature of divine justice as revealed in the Scriptures. God is both the Creator and the maker of a covenant in which a people, Israel, are created and transformed by the divine promise made to Abraham and to his descendants. God has been wondrously providential, never failing to provide for Israel's needs. It is for these deeds that God is praised as "just" and "righteous" toward Israel. Clearly such justice is not repayment of a debt owed but a faithful meeting of the needs of all creatures. Following St. Thomas, Pieper declares that "by virtue of creation first arises the possibility of saying 'Something is my due.' "[14] The dignity of human beings resides in the fact that God has created them.

God's justice is not an impartial rendering of judgments for transgressions of the law; rather, it is giving to all persons what they need in order to be faithful partners of the covenant. Toward that end divine righteousness is manifested both in the championing of the poor against the greed of the rich and in the chastisement of the exploiters in order that they might repent and reknit bonds of community. For the Israelites, imitation of Yahweh's justice meant recognizing that they existed in a

> web of relationships—king with people, judge with complainants, family with tribe and kinfolk, the community with the resident alien and suffering in their midst and all with the covenant of God—in which life is played out.[15]

Justice is foremost "fidelity to the demands of a relationship."[16] The enactment of justice aims at the solidarity of the community by seeing to it that the cries of its members do not go unheeded.

The demands of justice are most passionately revealed in the Hebrew Scriptures as concern for the poor. The strongest moral condemnations in the prophetic literature were reserved for those who exploited the weak and the poor. The prophet Amos warns of the futility of the temple sacrifices of the rich as long as they exploit the poor. Speaking for Yahweh, Amos cries out:

> I hate, I despise your feasts, I take no delight in your solemn assemblies. . . . But let justice roll down like waters and righteousness like an ever-flowing stream (Am 5:21, 24).

Likewise, Jeremiah admonishes: "Thus says the Lord: Do justice and righteousness, and deliver from the hand of the oppressor him who has been robbed. And do no wrong or violence to the alien, the fatherless and the widow" (Jer 22:3-4).

As a divine attribute justice seeks the good of all in order that all of creation may be reknit. For this reason it is not possible to separate God's justice from God's mercy. God's mercy (*chesed*), sings the psalmist, endures forever. Merton calls God's *chesed*

> a gratuitous mercy that considers no fitness, no worthiness, and no return. It is the way the Lord looks upon the guilty and with His look makes them at once innocent. . . . It is the love by which He married to mankind, so that if humanity is faithless to Him it must still always have a fidelity to which to return: that is His own fidelity.[17]

Justice is most itself that is attended by the quality of heart called mercy. Aquinas declared that "mercy without justice is the mother of dissolution, and justice without mercy is cruelty."[18] Justice stays the hand of cruelty, but alone it cannot produce community. Hence, in the Jewish and Christian traditions, the work of justice cannot reach its goal without the work of love. In the Jewish tradition the saint is the *chasid*, the instrument of divine mercy. The justice practiced by the merciful person excludes the desire for punishment and is not (thinly) veiled vengeance. Without the quality of mercy claims of justice are infected with the desire to "get even" or "settle a score." In its fullest sense justice requires "partiality" in the sense of demanding attention to the particularity of all the parties in situations where injustice must be undone. Only in one of its forms, legal justice, does the goal of impartiality apply.

Celie and the Reknitting of Community

We will offer an example of the rendering of justice by considering how one woman responded as victim to the brutality of sexism and racism. In her 1983 Pulitzer prize winning novel, *The Color Purple*, Alice Walker tells the story of Celie, a black woman who has known only subjection and deprivation. Celie's story, a fictional account, has countless sequels in the annals of the black struggle for justice. As her story begins, Celie has already been raped by "Pa" twice. Twice she has been made pregnant and twice the children she bears are secreted away from her. Then, "spoilt" as she is, Celie is delivered over to "Mr. _____" (her only way of referring to him) to a life of connubial slavery. His response to his own emasculation by white society is to subjugate her.

The catalyst in Celie's journey to self-respect and freedom is Shug Avery, a sensuous singer of the blues, who delivers Celie from a womb of shame into the light of the creation's loveliness where she is able to see her own. Strengthened by Shug's affection and respect, Celie is able to get off her knees and "enter into the creation." Suddenly the blinders are gone (you have to "git man off your eyeball before you can see anything a' tall," she says[19]) and it is as if she had new eyes for admiring the goodness and beauty of the creation and new courage to claim it as her birthright. Celie takes her stand against Mr. _____. The setting is Shug's announcement that she is leaving for Memphis and that Celie is going with her. Celie relates the drama of the exodus scene:

> Over my dead body, "Mr" say.
> You satisfied that what you want, Shug say, cool as clabber.
> He look over at me. I thought you was finally happy, he say. What wrong now?
> You a lowdown dog is what's wrong, I say. It's time to leave you and enter into the creation. And your dead body just the welcome mat I need.[20]

Celie's departing words are delivered with the vigor of the Israelite prophets: "Until you do right by me, everything you touch will crumble. You better stop talking because all I'm telling you ain't coming just from me. . . . The jail you plan for me is the one in which you will rot." Her final curse is replete with the truth of their lives: "Anything you do to me, already done to you."[21]

Mr. _____ is ravaged by a fitful depression and finds relief only when he acknowledges his guilt and begins to make restitution to Celie. But in time Celie returns. Having claimed her due and discovered her goodness she is able to bring "Albert" into the light of the creation with her.

He now has new eyes for her, causing Celie to say, "It begin to look like he got a lot of feeling hind his face."[22] Shorn of the pretense of being a spouse he now proves capable for the first time of friendship with Celie. As they grow old they spend their days on the porch sewing. In addition to the cloth with which they work they are stitching their lives together and joining the good creation. Albert (whom Celie can now refer to by his given name) finally says, "I think us here to wonder. The more I wonder, the more I love."[23]

Like many other black women in America, it is by Celie's emerging strength that the cycle of injustice is finally broken. Celie demands her due and pulls herself up from subjection. Her struggle transforms everybody's lives and relationship—beginning with Mr. _____.

This brief account of Walker's novel, while only a glimpse of its richness, suggests the power of justice to create community by connecting us with the goodness of our own lives and the goodness of one another. Celie is able to demand justice because she has seen the truth and has the courage to quit her prison. The justice she exacts is not vengeance. The truth with which she confronts Mr. _____ and the debt she demands be paid are the source of healing for the festering wounds of their lives and relationship. The final scene of *The Color Purple* is the reunion of Celie's family. The long separations and estrangements are over and now all are together and at peace with one another. It is the Fourth of July and one of the youngsters asks what that means. The answer comes "White folks busy celebrating their independence from England. So most black folks don't have to work. Us can spend the day celebrating each other."[24] Indeed this is the ultimate vision of justice: being able to celebrate one another. Justice in its variety of forms makes friendship possible.

The justice Celie sought was ultimately neither venge-

ance nor a declaration of independence from her oppressor. She left Albert but she also returned as the bringer of
mercy, the *chasid*, to heal him. Indeed, her justice proved to
be reconciling for all because mercy was its "second act."

Whether on behalf of others or ourselves, justice confronts us with a demand. We must respond to the claims of
others or deny both their need and their personhood; we
must claim our own human dignity or be made a party to
the frustration of our own personhood. David Harned defines justice as "enabling the other to be his own master."[25]
Justice demands that we neither acquiesce in the exploitation of others nor allow ourselves to be exploited and
desecrated. As Christians, we hold that the work of human
justice is finally imitation of the nature and activity of God—
as is also true for the virtue of love. Since love and justice
are both attributes of God we cannot rank one as higher
than the other. Justice enacts what love motivates. Love
elevates justice above a disguised form of self-service or
maintenance of the status quo that we may regard others as
genuinely other and deserving of our respect .

Like any example we might have chosen to illustrate
justice "in action," this one has its limitations. We mention
them here because it is important that justice not be misun-
derstood. In Celie we encounter an individual taking direct
action against another individual responsible for human
oppression. In fact, injustice is often far less visible (and far
less susceptible to being remedied) because it resides more
in institutional structures than in explicit human behavior.
While structural injustice requires no less of a personal response, the nature of the response will need to go beyond
changing the terms of interpersonal relationships. We are
required to work for justice on many fronts, seeking to
reform social, economic, and legal structures that oppress
people. This we will see in Martin Luther King's story below.

Celie's is nonetheless a reminder of the kind of vision and strength we need to resist injustice—with justice and mercy. Like Celie, our success at bringing about justice needs as its context an ever greater awareness of the goodness of God.

3. Hope, Patience, and Courage

> We rejoice in our suffering, knowing that suffering produces endurance, and endurance produces character, and character produces hope, and hope does not disappoint us, because God's love has been poured into our hearts through the Holy Spirit which has been given to us (Rom 5:3–5).

The great paradox of our condition as creatures is our simultaneous yearning to know more and our limited capacity for realizing that "more" by our own efforts. The fall represents our attempt to "storm the barricades" to obtain the knowledge possessed by God and our self-defeat and despair when we could not. The virtue of hope is our reassurance that we have indeed been created to glory in knowledge of God and the creation. But we shall receive such knowledge not "on demand" but as God's gracious gift. Pieper speaks of God's reality as a "brightness" illuminating the whole of creation with such intensity that eyes such as ours, unaccustomed to such light, cannot see. Hence, with St. Thomas he calls hope "the condition of our existence as a knowing subject."[26] We cannot rest with what appears to us as the real, for the depths and the heights of the real, the riches of the creation and its Maker, have yet to impress themselves upon our consciousness. Hope, then, is a fundamental religious response in which we acknowledge our limits and pray to be granted "more" of God.

The basis of Christian hope lies in what God has already done and promises to bring to completion in the future. In the Christian tradition the ground of hope is the story of the God who chose me in the distant past, named me in my mother's womb, who loves me still and promises to "make all things new." Christians look forward "to the creation of what does not yet exist, the initiation of relationships the self has not yet sought to achieve. . . ."[27] "Looking forward to" does not mean projecting our hope into the distant future. We must live the present with the expectation that God is breaking in to surprise us in ways we can hardly fathom. Hope for what is "not yet" elevates rather than devalues the present. It cannot be otherwise: for reliance upon a future that is unbridgeably distant from the present would have us despair of the present and every day henceforward as well. In order to understand the object of hope rightly we must not be victim of a so-called distinction between the "real" and the "ideal." Ideals are like mirages: they are never attainable and we soon tire of seeking such unsubstantial "realities." The object of our hope is not an "ideal" world. In *Theology of Hope* Jurgen Moltmann says that what is hoped for is not "idealistic." He believes:

> Hope alone is to be called 'realistic,' because it alone takes seriously the possibilities with which all reality is fraught. It does not take things as they happen to stand or lie, but as progressing, moving things with possibilities of change.[28]

These future possibilities are beyond our imagining.

For hope-filled people, there is great appreciation for the world around them because they see it as the site of the divine creative process. The world and their eyes for seeing it are being renewed. God's gift of hope comes in many forms. Shug Avery comes bearing it to Celie in teaching her to "wonder at" the world's beauty and eventually her own. When she can wonder at a field of purple and the golden hues of the setting sun she can begin to imagine the glories which the Creator of it has in store for her. From new hope comes Celie's emancipation.

Martin Luther King, Jr. and the Hope of a People

The virtue of hope is profoundly exemplified by the civil rights movement in the U.S. during the 1950s and 1960s which was inspired largely by the leadership of Martin Luther King, Jr. King was able to inspire thousands of black people to commit themselves to campaigns of non-violent resistance by tapping the deep wells of hope which have long nourished black spirituality. His wife, Coretta Scott King, wrote of him: "Remember him as a man who refused to lose faith in the ultimate redemption of mankind."[29] It was that conviction which he activated in countless others who had not dared to hope. All were enabled to sing "we shall overcome" with the unwavering hope that God was indeed doing something wonderfully new in Montgomery, Selma, Birmingham, and across the U.S. to renew the face of the earth.

When King came to Montgomery fresh from Boston University he found a black society groaning under injustice. But the groaning seemed to him the sound of birth. To white society's charge that he was disturbing Montgomery's racial peace, he replied that there was no peace in Montgomery but only "deadening passivity" that was the legacy of generations of injustice and the wholesale loss of black people's self-respect. King wrote that when Jesus said "I have not come to bring peace, but a sword" he was not legitimating violence but meant:

> I have not come to bring this old negative peace with its
> deadening passivity. I have come to lash out against
> such a peace. Whenever I come, a conflict is pre-
> cipitated between the old and the new. . . . I have come
> to bring a positive peace which is the presence of jus-
> tice, love, yea, even the Kingdom of God.[30]

While the campaigns King led remained faithful to their
non-violent commitments, the response of whites and other
blacks was often otherwise. White reaction was usually hos-
tile and sometimes violent. Younger black leadership wanted change even at the cost of violence if violence would
hasten it. The constituencies of black Baptists and Method-
ists will be remembered for carrying their religious faith into
the streets and reminding Christians everywhere of the
hope, courage, and patience to which all peoples of faith
must give testimony in their daily struggles.

The hope King demonstrated was grounded in his perception of what God was doing, and not in what human
beings were alone capable of knowing or doing. What could
be hoped for was known only to the God of infinite sur-
prises. The possibilities of freedom and racial harmony
were more than any political strategy or program could produce. Yet the prospects did not reside in a distant world but
in the transformation of this one. Human beings could only
hope to become God's worthy instruments in the redemptive process by prayerful discernment of God's activity.

King thoroughly rejected the view of Christianity (and
Marx's critique) as an opiate by which to endure this world
without challenging its injustice. He wrote:

> Religion deals with both earth and heaven, both time
> and eternity. . . . It seeks not only to integrate men with
> God but to integrate men with men and each man with
> himself. . . . Any religion that professes to be concerned

with the souls of men and is not concerned with the
slums that damn them, the economic conditions that
strangle them, and the social conditions that cripple
them is a dry as dust religion.[31]

King was instrumental in awakening southern blacks from
their quietist endurance of indignity to reclaim their human
respect. In the words of James McClendon, King was

a crucial factor in the awakening toward freedom of
Black America, because he gave his people *hope.* By
providing a new idea . . . and by raising the level of
expectation in Blacks, King produced "a deep ground-
swell of anticipation" during the late fifties. Thus filled
with hope, men acted, whether in King's way or in other
ways, to end the long night of repression.[32]

The kinds of attitudes and the brand of activism which
King forged in his freedom campaigners is a reflection of
the hope in which he (and they) were grounded. King refused to wrest justice from the white community by force.
For the future God has in store could not be taken by storm.
The capacity for non-violence which King fostered in himself and his followers was founded on the conviction that
through the power of suffering love human beings could
cooperate in the realization of God's justice in the world.
King's confidence was unshakable that "the universe was
on the side of justice."[33] King spoke of "cosmic com-
panionship" in the struggle for racial justice. He envisioned
himself and his fellow campaigners cooperating with the
"creative force in the universe that works to bring the dis-
connected aspects of reality into a harmonious whole."[34]
This was more than wishful thinking about what the world
might be like. It was, rather, unshakable confidence in the
nature of God and in God's ultimate power over the course

of human history. Justice will indeed come to pass, in time as well as eternity, on earth as in heaven.

For this kind of hope to be a living reality it must translate into the virtues of patience and courage. For patience is the willingness to suffer in order that what is hoped for may be brought to birth. The advice of whites to blacks (often echoed by fearful black churchmen) not to push too fast for change but to "have patience" is a corruption of the virtue of patience. King insisted that blacks must be radically impatient with conditions that deny them their birthright of self-respect—lest they be a party to it. Authentic patience is the determination to resist evil actively and non-violently. Such patience means courageously confronting evildoers but refusing to "repay evil with evil." Such patience is grounded on imitation of Jesus whose disarmed life and way of the cross were redemptive. Such patience makes us capable of resisting the temptation to become fanatical and destructive in order to make things "come out right." Hope is the horizon and patience is the step-by-step progress toward it.

Patience is learning to bear with situations, especially those that involve suffering. Real change is a painfully slow process. Rather than seizing opportunities for quick victories and extorting concessions, King and his followers acquired the patience necessary to change the pervasive social attitudes in which both whites and blacks had for generations been imprisoned. The ability to act rather than react requires that we see our lives as part of a process. Learning to be patient is a spiritual discipline, for in the enactment of this virtue we are put in touch with the spiritual energy which will make our actions bear the fruit of love. For the thousands of Montgomery blacks who walked to work for more than a year rather than ride segregated buses change did finally come. It was the fruit of their patience, their creative non-violent strategies, their prayer, and their capacity for loving their oppressors. The real victory for King and the thousands he led was in their deeper learning of the virtues through which to be more faithful witnesses to the ways of God in the world. The victory extends to the rest of the church who have seen in them the pathway to being more fully the people of God.

4. Vision

We have considered a number of virtues and the divine *caritas* which makes them possible and directs them toward friendship with God. The cardinal virtue we have failed to mention which can yet shed light on the Christian life is the virtue of perceptiveness, classically called prudence.[35] Both the ancient philosophers and the classical Christian writers stressed the need for wisdom in practical matters. Cicero discussed three faculties necessary for practical wisdom: memory of the past, understanding of the present, and foresight toward the future. Aquinas described this key virtue as the power to be "rightly disposed with regard to ends" and to recognize the means "suitably ordained to that due end."[36]

Iris Murdoch, moral philosopher and novelist, writes that while we are meant to know the truth and live according to it, "our minds are continually active, fabricating an anxious, usually self-preoccupied, often falsifying *veil* which partially conceals the world. . . ."[37] For Murdoch, the virtues enable us "to pierce the veil of selfish consciousness and join the world as it really is."[38] Likewise, Josef Pieper speaks of the need to silence our "egoistic 'interests' in order that [we] may perceive the truth of real things . . . so that reality itself may guide [us] to the proper means of realizing [our] goal."[39] Aquinas emphasized the importance of reason for guiding our appetites. Guided by the eye of reason we are able to perfect the other cardinal virtues as well: being just means seeing and honoring the claims that others make on us; being temperate means not allowing inordinate desire for pleasure to blind us to reality; being courageous means being able to put ourselves at personal risk in pursuit of the truth.

Perceptiveness is not easily learned. As we noted in Chapter Three, our reason and our will are distorted by sin. Yet though our own powers of moral perception are quite dim, when we receive the gift of divine wisdom we are filled with light. Recall the clarity of vision which took hold of Jeremiah and Amos, Dorothy Day, Celie, and Martin Luther King, Jr., giving them the insight into what they needed to do. They were counter-cultural and their actions were "imprudent" in the eyes of many. Indeed, their moral perceptiveness places them in the company of Jesus, whose cross was "foolishness" to the worldly wise. Jesus is the wisdom of God. His life illumined the ways of God in the world. The kind of perceptiveness necessary in the Christian life is ultimately a gift of divine wisdom. For our part, we prepare to receive it by seeking continually, prayerfully, to discern what God is doing. The attainment of such perceptiveness is the unified spiritual and moral task of the Christian community.

As the gathering of those who seek the kingdom, the church anticipates the future incorporation of the entire human race under the loving reign of God. Its mission is to pray earnestly for God's full saving presence in human history and by its way of love to offer the world a glimpse or a foretaste of the kingdom. The church's ritual and sacramental life are reminders to all who participate in them of the offer of transformation given by and through Jesus. Its practice of the virtues is for the purpose of announcing what kingdom life is like. The virtues which it possesses are not signs of its superiority but of the power of God working in human history. The virtues of compassion, justice, patience, courage and hope being enacted by the community are signs of the life under the reign of God. The church itself is not the kingdom. It is provisional, existing in order to point to the kingdom and to encourage and welcome others to join in its pilgrimage toward the kingdom. The church is not the destination, but the company of those who seek to be schooled in the kingdom way of life.

Conclusion

Certain questions continually confront to us: How can we "live up to" the life we have been given? How can we use our freedom responsibly? How much control over our lives do we really have? The latter is perhaps *the* question, underlying and fundamental to the moral questions of living well and responsibly. The way we answer the question of how much we are in control of our lives is also critical to our spiritual formation. The final chapter of our examination of spirituality and morality raised the question of our use of power. Before moving to three final observations about the relationship between Christian morality and spirituality, we must briefly consider the matter of human control.

To raise the question of human control means that we are self-reflective enough to have some control over our situation. We know that we have the power of reason and the will to deliberate and act. But our capacity of deliberation, like our senses, is limited. Just as we cannot see very far, nor very well in the dark, nor in more than one direction at a time, we are often unsure of what we should do—or, in H. Richard Niebuhr's expression, how we should interpret and respond to "what is happening to us." Our freedom is limited not only by the limits of our faculties but also by the partial blinding we have inflicted upon ourselves. Our sinfulness is reflected in our preference for a fantasy world in which we dominate everything and everyone on the horizon. As the story of the fall in Genesis illustrates, we have succumbed to the temptation to dominate everyone and everything around us.

Ironically, while the evangelists of technology are telling us that we have unprecedented control over the environment and can expect to have even more, we are actually experiencing less and less control. And in the age of a communication "revolution" we are often very lonely, feeling unconnected to and unsupported by family, friends, and community. We may be feeling powerless and hopeless about the things that matter most: intimate relationships, healthy communities and peace.

Christianity is grounded in the conviction that God's creative and redemptive power makes it possible for us to live "out of control," without the fear—even with our limits and our sinfulness—that we will be destroyed. The divine power has "broken into" our lives in ways we could not have anticipated. In the person Jesus, God's anointed one, we find encouragement and assurance that if we are willing to acknowledge our radical need, God will give us more than we could ever imagine. In the words of St. Paul, "eyes have not seen nor ears heard, what God has in store for those who love him" (1 Cor 2:9, quoting Isaiah 64:4).

Spirituality is the process of discovering God's power in our lives in order that we might become holy. The power of the Spirit is conferred on every Christian at baptism. As a discipline, spirituality is learning how to wait, hopefully and prayerfully. The fruit of such waiting is our emergence from our loneliness, now enabled to befriend one another. Life's stages and stations are all opportunities to experience greater love of God through love of one another.

It is appropriate to speak of Christian spirituality and morality as learning how to be church. For the very existence of the church reveals essential features of Christian spirituality and morality. First of all, spiritual and moral growth are communal affairs in which growth occurs with and through others. The church is not a society with which we may or may not choose to affiliate when we have become believers. It is not a support group which may or may not be useful in our faith journeys. Rather it is the ingathering of those who have had the experience of belief in Jesus. We believe that Jesus is present in that community. Its word, sacraments, and work in the world offer us the promise of deeper encounter with Jesus. Entry into the life of the church means incorporating ourselves into the transforming life of Jesus Christ. The call to be *a holy people* reminds us that the call to holiness is not issued to individuals but to a community of persons. We are to join one another in a shared response. That the holiness to which we are called is meant to be a communal experience rather than only an individual one is a reminder that holiness is not something to be attained and possessed by and for ourselves. Rather, the encounter with God is a gift which when shared is received more fully.

The existence of the church testifies, second, that salvation occurs in this world, reflecting God's love of the world and refusal to abandon it. Christians proclaim that by the incarnation redemption is no longer "worlds away" but is going on by means of the one who shared our humanity. The church is a continuation of God's saving presence in the world, incarnated in human beings who have committed their freedom to the power of God's reign. It is the "earthen vessel" in which all flesh is to be divinely transformed. As such, the church's very existence affirms that the world is redeemable. The realization that the church is a weak human steward of God's power that so often has been unfaithful to its mission reminds us of the continual need for Christians themselves—before all others—to repent, to be more deeply converted, and to reform their own community in order to be drawn to deeper life.

Third, the existence of the church reminds us of its task in the world. The mission of the church is not to serve itself but to be a servant community that announces the kingdom by feeding the hungry, comforting the afflicted, welcoming the stranger, and championing those too weak to have their voices heeded and their personhood honored. In the story of the last judgment (Mt 25) we are told that Jesus' disciples will discern the Master himself when they have acted as a servant community on behalf of these suffering people. We are most conspicuously "being church" not at those moments when we gather together but when we are dispersed in the world doing the work of Jesus. For the church does not lead us out of the world but into deeper awareness of it in order that we might have fuller life. In *The Company of Strangers* Parker Palmer writes:

> I have been helped by thinking of the church as a "school of the Spirit," a place where God is continually drawing me out of myself into the larger life. A school has familial features, an ethos of caring for its students. But a school will also correct and upbraid and uproot us, introduce us to the strange and unfamiliar, teach us a truth larger than our own.[1]

This brings us to three final "words" about the bringing together of our spiritual and our moral journeys. The first is a reminder of the purpose of the spiritual disciplines. The second and third reiterate the danger and the promise, respectively, of self-consciously uniting our spiritual and moral aspirations.

1. "Good Works, Good Works"

St. Teresa tried to describe to her religious community her experience of God. She used the image of a "spiritual marriage" to describe what she had received from God. Although such a description might seem to describe a mystical flight that carried her away from the world, it is interesting to hear her very concrete advice to her sisters. The contemplative life, she wrote, must give "birth always of good works, good works."[2] Indeed through her intimacy with God, Teresa was empowered to carry out works of justice and mercy. The sublime encounter with God made not only for personal healing but also for healing the woundedness of others. A contemporary member of Teresa's religious community, Vilma Seelaus describes the use of the spiritual power we are given in terms of healing others:

> We must touch each other's woundedness. But we must get beyond the woundedness and be transformed. To see ourselves as "different" is to cut ourselves off from others—which is a form of self-possession. Unless I'm related to others—all others, the flow of humanity—I'm cut off from the energy source. I have to hear the cry of the poor and respond in my own way, one way or another.[3]

These words challenge us to break down the walls of self-possession and to respond, "one way or another," to the cry of others' pain. The power of the Spirit, when it is authentically present, is contagious. That is, those who have received it want also to empower those who are marginalized. True contemplatives, living as they do in their monasteries, are not cut off from the world but care intensely about its well-being. Teresa regularly reminded her sisters that prayer without the practice of the virtues was impossible.[4] She warned against a form of spirituality that would "build castles in the air" and urged a very practical sort of mortification:

> . . . during the little time that life lasts . . . let us offer the Lord interiorly and exteriorly the sacrifice we can. His majesty will join it with that which He offered on the Cross to the Father for us.[5]

Teresa is suggesting service to others that is inspired by the life and death of Jesus.

What might be called "spiritual biographies" are also stories of people doing the work of the kingdom through the practice of the virtues. Prudence and compassion, justice and mercy, patience and courage, humility and hope are indeed the marks of the power of the Spirit, a power not our own which makes us free and fit for friendship with God and with one another. These are the stories of what it means to "be church."

2. Against Perfectionism: On Not Casting the First Stone

As the U.S. Catholic bishops anticipated it would, the pastoral letter *The Challenge of Peace* (1983) has raised many questions. One such question concerns what the Church has "traditionally" taught about the use of force against aggressor nations. The letter summarizes both the "just war" and the pacifist traditions without claiming either to be the definitive Catholic stance. Some object that the just war teaching is clearly the Catholic answer. Others, influenced by the Catholic peace movement, lament that by not speaking out more stridently against war and in favor of non-violence, the bishops have not been prophetic enough. For their part, the bishops see the question as unsettled and "in process." The very writing of a pastoral letter concerning public policy on national defense issues has raised other questions. Some have questioned whether the bishops have gone beyond their competence (although the bishops self-consciously write as moral teachers rather than as defense experts). Others see the Church's commitment to influencing the political process as a capitulation to an "evil" military-industrial-economic system that needs to be repudiated rather than conditionally tolerated as the bishops have done, apparently in the interest of not alienating large segments of the U.S. population—Catholics included.

It is especially tempting to join the protest against the bishops from a "perfectionist" point of view which sees the Church committed to peace and fears that anything less than a prophetic stance will not help to halt the runaway arms race. After all, we as Christians believe that power is to be used in the service of compassion and with humility rather than in the service of unbridled nationalism. Entering into dialogue with political structures which take violence for granted may seem to be compromising those convictions. Does remaining "pure" and steadfast mean refusing political engagement?

I have raised the issues of the "peace" pastoral and of entering into moral controversies (other controversial issues such as abortion might also have been raised) in order to address the danger of perfectionism. Spiritual growth includes the temptation to view others as less spiritual and to live apart from them. From such a "perfectionist" perspective it is compromising to settle for less than perfect systems. Like those who will not engage the bishops because they believe that national defense is "none of their business," spiritual elitists will not bother because they fear the compromising of their beliefs. There is more of the latter tendency in us than we like to admit. And our motivation for it may well need chastening. May not opting for the prophetic over the political response—instead of recognizing the legitimacy of both—represent the failure to recognize the goodness of those who do not live as I live and believe what I believe? Obviously spiritual growth is meant to unite us rather than cut us off from others.

Are those who differ from us and those who we find difficult not the very ones we are called to love? Spiritual achievement, if it means anything, means that we are better able to see how similar to one another we really are. As Merton recalled, one of his greatest spiritual insights was the recognition of his likeness to all those he observed on a busy street corner of Louisville during one of his trips outside his monastery. Merton coped with and often warned his fellow monks of the dangers of spiritual pride.

3. Living the Contradictions

At times we may feel that spirituality and our everyday lives are poles apart. The demands of the active life and the solitude necessary for contemplation may seem in permanent conflict. Pursuing one may seem to preclude pursuing the other. Resolving moral issues and becoming decent moral actors may seem to place us in a different world of experience from the world in which the spiritual seeker lives. Consider some apparent dichotomies. The commitment to live simply and even renounce material pursuits may seem at odds with focusing one's energies on greater productivity so that more can share in the goods of the earth. Spiritual growth appears to be a luxury for the few whose needs are well met in a world in which whole peoples are hungry and without social justice. These seeming oppositions are challenging. The challenge is not to choose one as the better way and deny the other as an unworthy pursuit but to live within the tension of the two. To decide that one way of life is "too worldly" or that the other is "too utopian" is to close ourselves off from much of reality. Our greatest growth is to be found in living the tension by holding together these poles as best we can. Whatever anomaly there seems to be between the spiritual life and the moral life will only be resolved by striving for holy worldliness and viewing both holiness and worldliness part and parcel of what it means to call oneself Christian.

Notes

Introduction

1. Thomas Merton, *Seeds of Contemplation* (Norfolk: New Directions, 1949), p. 13.

2. *Ibid.*, p. 22.

3. The fact that we have far to go is reflected in a recent (and widely used) textbook in moral theology. In its concluding pages the author speaks of the "three distinct tasks" of Christian living: developing an ethical commitment; nourishing it by means of an "inner spirituality"; giving it expression through liturgical participation. Noting that not everything could be said in the foregoing two hundred pages, the author acknowledges: "We have not spoken of a most potent theme: the ascesis of love which must surely play a role in the successful living of the Christian life": Timothy E. O'Connell, *Principles for a Catholic Morality* (New York: Seabury, 1978), p. 209.

4. *Seeds*, p. 21.

1. Jesus, Alpha and Omega

1. *A Future for the Historical Jesus* (Nashville: Abingdon Press, 1971), p. 245.

2. *A Community of Character: Toward a Constructive Christian Social Ethic* (Notre Dame: University of Notre Dame Press, 1981), p. 45.

133

3. *Jesus: The Compassion of God* (Wilmington: Michael Glazier, Inc., 1983), p. 83.

4. *The Wound of Knowledge: Christian Spirituality from the New Testament to Luther and John of the Cross* (Atlanta: John Knox Press, 1980), pp. 3–4.

5. *The Founder of Christianity* (New York: Macmillan Publishing Company, 1970), p. 171.

6. "Mysticism in the Nuclear Age," from *The Ascent to Truth* (Viking Press, 1951); reprinted in *A Thomas Merton Reader* (New York: Doubleday Image Books, 1974), pp. 371–78, at pp. 377–78.

7. *Christ and the Moral Life* (New York: Harper & Row, 1968), p. 183.

8. *The Peaceable Kingdom: A Primer in Christian Ethics* (Notre Dame: University of Notre Dame Press, 1983), pp. 75–76.

9. *The Heart of the World: A Spiritual Catechism* (New York: Crossroad, 1981), pp. 71–72.

10. *The Wound of Knowledge*, pp. 7, 10.

11. *The Transformation of Man: A Study of Conversion and Community* (New York: Paulist Press, 1967), p. 120.

12. *Ibid.*, p. 107.

13. *Ibid.*, pp. 108–109.

14. *Ibid.*, p. 111.

15. "Contemplation and Action: Personal Spirituality/World Reality," in *Dimensions of Contemporary Spirituality*, ed. Francis Eigo, O.S.A. (Villanova: Villanova University Press, 1982), pp. 143–162, at p. 145.

16. *Ibid.*

17. *Ibid.*

18. *The Quest for the Historical Jesus*, translated by W. Montgomery from the first German edition, *Von Reimarus zu Wrede*, 1906 (New York: The Macmillan Company, 1968), p. 401.

2. The Spiritual Journey

1. Editor's introduction to *Company*, Vol. 1, No. 3 (April 1984), p. 1.

2. Samuel Beckett, *Waiting for Godot* (New York: Grove Press, Inc. 1954). The play has been staged by many companies since its opening in a Paris theatre in 1948. A prominent American production of the play in the 1960s was acted by inmates of the San Quentin, California, prison.

3. Simone Weil, *Waiting for God*, trans. by Emma Craufurd, with an introduction by Leslie Fiedler (New York: Putnam, 1951), p. 133.

4. T.S. Eliot, *Four Quartets*, East Coker, III (New York: Harcourt Brace Jovanovich, 1943).

5. Henri Nouwen, *Out of Solitude* (Notre Dame: Ave Maria Press, 1974), pp. 13–14.

6. Thomas Keating, *The Heart of the World*, p. 48.

7. St. Teresa of Avila, *The Life*, trans. by Kieran Kavanaugh, O.C.D. and Otilio Rodriguez, O.C.D. (Washington, D.C.: Institute of Carmelite Spirituality, 1976), Ch. 22.

8. Keating, p. 47.

9. *The Way of a Pilgrim* (authorship unknown), trans. from the Russian by R.M. French (London: SPCK, 1930, 1952).

10. Weil, pp. 133–34.

11. Merton, *Seeds of Contemplation*, p. 34.

12. *Ibid.*

13. St. Teresa of Avila, *The Life*, Ch. 11.

14. Erik Erikson, *Identity: Youth and Crisis* (New York: Norton, 1968), p. 92.

15. Vilma Seelaus, unpublished lecture delivered at Seminar on Carmelite Spirituality, St. Mary's College, Notre Dame, Indiana, June 1985.

16. Florida Scott-Maxwell, *The Measure of My Days* (New York: Knopf, 1968) quoted in Colman McCarthy, *Inner Companions* (Washington, D.C.: Acropolis Books, 1975) pp. 221–22.

17. Evelyn E. and James D. Whitehead, *Christian Life Patterns: The Psychological Challenges and Religious Invitations of Adult Life* (Garden City: Doubleday and Company, 1979), p. 45.

18. Evelyn and James Whitehead, p. 45.

19. Thomas Keating, p. 12.

20. Thomas Merton, "Marxism and Monastic Perspectives,"

a talk delivered in Bangkok, Thailand, on December 10, 1968; reprinted in *The Asian Journal of Thomas Merton* (New York: New Directions Books, 1973), p. 338.

3. The Christian Moral Life

1. "Decree on Priestly Formation," n. 16, in *The Documents of Vatican II*, ed. Walter M. Abbott, S.J. (Chicago: Follett Publishing Company, 1966), p. 452.

2. Thomas Gilby, commenting on the *Prima Secunda*, Questions 1–5, in the Blackfriars edition of the *Summa Theologiae* (Washington, D.C.: Blackfriars, 1969), Vol. 16, p. 1.

3. *The Responsible Self* (New York: Harper and Row, 1963), p. 56.

4. *Ibid.*, p. 60.

5. *Ibid.*, p. 60–61.

6. *Ibid.*, p. 67.

7. Thomas Merton, *Seeds of Contemplation*, p. 10.

8. *Ibid.*

9. *Ibid.*, pp. 10–11.

10. *Summa Theologiae*, 1–2, q. 6, a. 1.

11. *S. T.*, 1–2, q. 6, prol.

12. *S. T.*, 1–2, q. 1, a. 1.

13. *S. T.*, 1–2, q. 6, prol.

14. Hauerwas, *Vision and Virtue*, (Notre Dame: Fides Publishers, 1974), p. 41.

15. *Ibid.*, p. 40.

16. See Nouwen, *Creative Ministry* (New York: Doubleday Image Books, 1979).

17. *Vision and Virtue*, pp. 41–42.

18. Callahan, "Minimalist Ethics: On the Pacification of Morality," *Hastings Center Report* (October 1981) and reprinted in *Vice and Virtue in Everyday Life*, Christina Hoff Sommers, ed. (New York: Harcourt Brace Jovanovich, 1985), pp. 636–652.

19. Jonathan Schell, *The Fate of the Earth* (New York: Knopf, 1982).

20. Thomas Merton, "A Body of Broken Bones," in *A*

Thomas Merton Reader (Garden City: Doubleday and Company, 1974), p. 321.

    21. *Ibid.*, p. 319.
    22. *Seeds*, pp. 30–31.
    23. *Seeds*, p. 32.

4. Power

    1. H. Richard Niebuhr, *Christ and Culture* (New York: Harper and Row, 1951), p. 27.
    2. "Two Kinds of Power," *The Criterion* Vol. 15, No. 1 (Winter, 1976), pp. 11–29.
    3. *Ibid.*, p. 13.
    4. *Ibid.*, p. 18.
    5. Thomas Merton, *Faith and Violence* (Notre Dame: University of Notre Dame Press, 1968), p. 220.
    6. *Ibid.*, p. 219.
    7. Tocqueville, *Democracy in America*, trans. George Lawrence, ed. J.P. Mayer (New York: Harper and Row, 1966), Vol. 2, Part 2, Ch. 13, p. 508.
    8. *Ibid.*
    9. Robert N. Bellah, Richard Madsen, William M. Sullivan, Ann Swidler, Steven M. Tipton, *Habits of the Heart: Individualism and Commitment in American Life* (New York: Harper and Row, 1985). The authors quote Tocqueville, *Democracy in America*, Vol. 2, Part 2, Ch. 2, p. 477.
    10. Bellah, *et al.*, p. 81.
    11. Sandel, *Liberalism and the Limits of Justice* (New York: Cambridge University Press, 1982).
    12. Tocqueville, p. 478.
    13. Mary Collins, O.S.B., "Community and Forgiveness," *New Catholic World*, Vol. 227, No. 1357 (January–February 1984), p. 14.
    14. *Ibid.*
    15. *Ibid.*, p. 13.
    16. *Ibid.*, p. 12.
    17. *Ibid.*, p. 13 (italics mine).

18. Philip J. Rossi, S.J., *Together Toward Hope: A Journey to Moral Theology* (Notre Dame: University of Notre Dame Press, 1983), p. 49.

19. In fact, the pacifist and "just war" positions maintained by members of the churches are both founded on suspicion of and reservation about the use of lethal force.

20. "The Grace of Doing Nothing," *Christian Century*, Vol. 49 (March 23, 1932) pp. 378–80, at p. 379.

21. Niebuhr's counsel is reminiscent of the climactic words of the story of King David's treachery to obtain Bathsheba for his wife. The prophet Nathan tells King David the story of a man of great wealth who nonetheless robs a poor shepherd of his only lamb. When David asks with great indignation "Who is that man?" Nathan asserts: "You are the man!" (2 Sam 12).

22. "The Grace of Doing Nothing," p. 379.

23. *Ibid.*, pp. 379–80.

24. "Must We Do Nothing?" *Christian Century*, 49 (March 30, 1932), pp. 415–417, at p. 417.

25. H. Richard Niebuhr, "The Only Way into the Kingdom," *Christian Century*, 49 (April 6, 1932), p. 447.

26. *Ibid.*

27. Thomas Merton, "A Body of Broken Bones," p. 322 (italics in the original).

28. Vilma Seelaus, "Contemplative Presence to God and to Creation," *Contemplative Review*, Vol. 11, No. 4 (Winter 1978), pp. 10–11.

29. Merton, *Seeds of Contemplation*, p. 7.

30. *Ibid.*

31. *Ibid.*, p. 6.

32. *Ibid.*, p. 32.

33. *The Transformation of Man*, p. 119.

5. The Habits of the Christian Life

1. *Summa Theologiae*, II–II, 23, 8.

2. *S.T.*, II–I, 62, 1.

3. *S.T.*, II–II, 90.

4. Merton, "A Body of Broken Bones," p. 320.

5. *Ibid.*, p. 323.

6. Dorothy Day, *The Long Loneliness* (New York: Curtis Books, 1952).

7. *Ibid.*, pp. 98–99.

8. *Ibid.*, p. 89.

9. *Ibid.*, p. 120.

10. *Ibid.*, p. 159.

11. *Ibid.*, p. 242.

12. *S.T.*, II–II, 62.

13. Josef Pieper, *The Four Cardinal Virtues* (New York: Harcourt Brace Jovanovich, 1965), cf. "Justice."

14. *Ibid.*, p. 46.

15. John R. Donahue, S.J., "Biblical Perspectives on Justice," in *The Faith That Does Justice* (New York: Paulist Press, 1977), pp. 69–112, at p. 69.

16. *Ibid.*

17. Thomas Merton, "The Good Samaritan," in *A Thomas Merton Reader*, pp. 348–356, at p. 353.

18. *S.T.*, II–II, 62.

19. Alice Walker, *The Color Purple* (New York: Washington Square Press, 1982), p. 179.

20. *Ibid.*, p. 181.

21. *Ibid.*, p. 187.

22. *Ibid.*, p. 239.

23. *Ibid.*, p. 247.

24. *Ibid.*, p. 250.

25. David Harned, *Faith and Virtue* (Philadelphia: United Church Press, 1973), p. 132.

26. *The Silence of Saint Thomas*, trans. by John Murray, S.J. and Daniel O'Connor (New York: Pantheon, 1957), p. 69.

27. Harned, p. 53.

28. Jurgen Moltmann, *Theology of Hope* (New York: Harper and Row, 1967), p. 25.

29. Preface to *The Trumpet of Conscience* (New York: Harper and Row, 1967), p. xii.

30. Martin Luther King, Jr., *Stride Toward Freedom* (New York: Harper and Row, 1958), p. 40.

31. *Ibid.*, p. 36.

32. *Biography as Theology* (Nashville: Abingdon Press, 1974), p. 71. McClendon is quoting Lerone Bennett, *What Manner of Man*, p. 90.

33. *Stride Toward Freedom*, p. 106.

34. *Ibid.*, p. 107.

35. Nowadays prudence connotes a timidity toward life or a straight-laced demeanor masking repressed desire. Because of the many negative associations with the word, it is advisable to substitute for it a term which connotes moral vision. I am indebted to my wife, Mary Beth Duffey, for among other things suggesting that the classical meaning of "prudence" is not sufficiently clear to modern readers to warrant using the word for what I am trying to describe and for helping me clarify how perception is indeed a Christian virtue.

36. *S.T.*, I–II, 57, 4 and 5.

37. "The Sovereignty of the Good," p. 84, quoted by Stanley Hauerwas in *Vision and Virtue* (Notre Dame: Fides Publishers, Inc., 1974), p. 33.

38. *Ibid.*, p. 93.

39. Josef Pieper, *The Four Cardinal Virtues*, p. 20.

Conclusion

1. *The Company of Strangers* (New York: Crossroads Publishing Company, 1981), pp. 123–124.

2. Quoted by John Welch, *Spiritual Pilgrims: Carl Jung and Teresa of Avila* (N.Y.: Paulist Press, 1982), p. 184.

3. Vilma Seelaus, Unpublished Lecture, delivered at St. Mary's College, Notre Dame, Indiana, June 1985.

4. Cf. *Interior Castle*, Part VII, Ch. 4, No. 11.

5. *Ibid.*, No. 15.